J.

CW00357937

3O AUG

BOOK LAUNCH
HAWICK TOWN HALL

Songs of Teviotdale
A Companion to the Hawick Songs

Ian W. Seeley

Published by Hawick Archaeological Society 2013

ISBN 978-0-9518647-5-3

Printed and bound for Hawick Archaeological Society

by Richardson & Son Printers,
Unit 7, Lochpark Industrial Estate, Hawick
www.richardsonprinters.com

2013

Cover photo by Lesley Fraser, ILF Imaging

Hawick Archaeological Society

www.airchieoliver.co.uk

Hawick Archaeological Society
and the author gratefully acknowledge the assistance
of the following in funding this publication;

The Ancient Order of Mosstroopers

Hawick Callants' Club

Hawick Sings

Hawick 1514 Club

Supporters of Hawick,
its Customs and Traditions Association

Scocha

FOREWORD

You hold in your hands the definitive guide to the songs of Hawick. It's the book about those words and tunes that needed to be written. While many earlier publications described individual songs and the people who created them, never before has there been so comprehensive a book. The author has been careful to check every fact. Now we have this "companion" to tell us everything we need to know about Hawick's musical traditions.

Few places in the world can boast such a volume of poetry written in its praise. The town of Hawick must be the square mile of the Earth's surface that is the most celebrated in song. Why that should be the case is baffling to non-Teries. So, one wouldn't expect that a man from the far north of Scotland (well, Fife at least!) would develop such a deep appreciation for Hawick's songs. But clearly, for Ian Seeley the music of Hawick has been intimately tied to his evolving love for the customs, traditions and landscape surrounding "the grey auld toon".

Seeley has become the modern custodian of Hawick's musical legacy. He is the successor to Adam Grant and Adie Ingles, who did so much to preserve and enhance our musical heritage. As well as playing and arranging existing songs, and writing new songs of his own, Seeley has also tirelessly researched the historical background of Hawick's music.

To use a phrase often heard at the Common Riding: "He is the right man in the right place at the right time". Ian Seeley has produced a remarkable contribution to celebrate Hawick's musical tradition. The depth of his feeling for these songs is palpable – strong opinions abound, but only because he genuinely cares. The Hawick songs are in the best hands here, and it is a pleasure to be led through them by this expert guide.

Douglas Scott, Vancouver, 2013

Adam Grant
The doyen of Hawick song

Adam L. Ingles
Arranger of the 1957 anthology

Ian W. Seeley
Editor of the 2001 anthology

Winning Combinations

J.E.D. Murray

Adam Grant

Adam N. McL. Colledge

Thomas Caldwell

Robert Hunter

Francis George Scott

All Their Own Work

Tom Ker

Ian W. Landles

Neil MacKay

Alan G. Brydon

David Finnie

(L – R) Iain H. Scott – President of Hawick Archaeological
Society, Henry S. Douglas – Chairman of song revision
committee 2001, with Ian W. Seeley

PREFACE

In 2000, Hawick Callants' Club decided to revise and enlarge *The Hawick Songs – A Complete Collection* – their landmark publication of 1957. Although it had been born in controversy, it was, nevertheless, an unqualified success which had the effect of stimulating interest in the Hawick songs and pointing the way to fresh creativity to such an extent that an enlarged edition was deemed to be both overdue and desirable.

A sub-committee, under the chairmanship of Ex-Acting Father Henry S. Douglas was convened with the remit of vetting and selecting new material and Ian Seeley was invited to be musical editor of the new volume. Besides editing the actual music and writing piano accompaniments as necessary, there was also a historical aspect to be considered, viz. the dating of authors, composers and arrangers. The latter was a precedent set by Adam Ingles some forty five years previously when, in 1955, he began compiling and arranging the 1957 volume. He followed this up in a paper given to Hawick Archaeological Society (1962) on the history of the songs and their creators. Following his death in 1991, his notes were published by the Society in booklet form and this has provided a starting point for the present text. It became apparent, however, that the *post mortem* Ingles publication was compromised by a number of omissions, mis-datings, printing errors and other historical inaccuracies. The present text endeavours to rectify these and expand the information on the basis of extant historical documentation. In other words, nothing is presented as fact if it cannot be substantiated. To this end, much of the reference material is given with the main text to obviate the need for constant reference to the back of the book. Such information as appears in Notes & Sources may be seen as auxiliary. Similarly, cross referencing has been employed extensively in order to spare the reader constant reference to an index. The alphabetical order of the entries is its own index.

History is always being revised and rewritten; what is produced here has all been re-researched, and while it is hoped that any historical errors will be few, or even non-existent, the author is sufficiently realistic to appreciate that he does not hold a monopoly on knowledge and would welcome correction and guidance should the need arise.

The Hawick songs, as a genre, are unique. The writer is confident that there exists no other place on the surface of the globe that has inspired such outpouring of poetical and musical expression. A report from *The Spectator* (reproduced in the *Hawick Express* 5/6/1963) observes – 'Surely Hawick must be among the most laureated towns in the land. It has proved to be a veritable nest of singing birds whose notes rise to a kind of clarion chorus when the Common Riding comes round. How comes it to be so? I venture to suggest that the beauty and historic interest of the Borderland has something to do with it.' Nor has this localised creativity been limited to natives of Hawick (Teries). Of forty three Hawick songs in the 2001 publication, thirteen sets of lyrics (30%) are by non-Teries while the statistic for the musical composition of nineteen song melodies is even higher (44%).

A number of what might be termed 'para-Hawick songs' have not been included in the main text; they do have a Hawick connection, but would not normally be standard fare at a Hawick Night. These include *Scotland Yet!* (words by Henry Scott Riddell, who lived at Flex just outside Hawick), *The Star O' Robbie Burns* (words by James Thomson), *The Hill Abuin Blawearie* (a personal tribute to his parents by Gordon Muir), *Auld Jock* and *Man O' Mony Pairts* (vocal sketches of local personalities with words and music by Alan Brydon). David Finnie's *The Old Man's Seat* is yet another example. This is a 'grey area' because there are songs already in the book which might also verge on this category – *The Lassie That Works In The Mill*, for example; is this really a Hawick song? *The Soft Lowland Tongue* (by William Sanderson of Peebles), though included in the anthology (simply because, for reasons he felt he could justify, Adam Ingles put it in) is not included here for the same reason that debars Matt McGinn's *The Rolling Hills Of The Border* – it is not a Hawick song.

Up to, and including, the ceremony of 1901, it was not unusual to have non-Hawick songs at the annual Colour Bussing. Teries, like all other Scots, had been singing traditional Scots songs and ballads long before the flowering of their own particular genre. It was not something they were going to discard readily, nor did they. (Scots traditional song had been in vogue in Eighteenth Century London, as attested by the outstanding success of William Thomson's anthology, *Orpheus Caledonius* of 1733, which, incidentally, includes *The Bonny Lass O' Branksome* – should it be in our anthology?). The last appearance of such at a Colour Bussing ceremony was *Scotland Yet!* in 1901, but it had also been on the programmes for 1887, 1888, 1891, 1893 and 1894. Other favourites were *The Flowers O' The Forest, Lock The Door, Lariston* and *The Auld Scots Sangs.* By the opening of the Twentieth Century, however, the Hawick-specific repertoire had seen such expansion as to obviate the use of traditional Scots songs. Today, we have a different problem. There are now so many Hawick songs, indeed, that concern is already being expressed in some quarters regarding the lack of usage of certain erstwhile late Victorian and early Twentieth Century favourites. Many communities would be happy to have such a 'problem'. Even as this resource goes to print, new songs are being written; an unusual 'problem' indeed for a very unusual, special, inspirational place. This text is all about that inspiration and the inspired.

Ian W. Seeley, Hawick, 2013

ACKNOWLEDGMENTS

The author gratefully acknowledges the invaluable assistance of

Australian High Commission, London

Drumlanrig St. Cuthbert's Primary School, Hawick

Dundee Teachers' Training College Archive,
Dundee University Archives

Edinburgh Central Library

Edinburgh Burials Registry,
Mortonhall Crematorium, Edinburgh

Educational Institute of Scotland, Edinburgh

Hawick Heritage Hub

Hawick Museum

Hawick Public Library

Moray House College Archive, Edinburgh University

Orkney Library and Archive, Kirkwall, Orkney

Registry of Genealogy, Scottish Borders Council,
Drumlanrig's Tower, Hawick

Scottish Borders Council Burials Registry, Hawick Town Hall

Strathclyde University Archives, Glasgow

Sydney Burials Registry, NSW, Australia

Yetholm School, Scottish Borders

Messrs. Robert Armstrong MBE, Kenneth Baxter,
Alan G. Brydon, Edward Czajka,
Ex-Acting Father Henry S. Douglas, David Finnie,
Peter Gentleman, the late David S. Gibb MBE,
George L. Goodfellow, Ex-Acting Father Tom Hartop,
David A. Hill, Andrew Lackenby, Ian W. Landles BEM,
James G. A. Letham, David Mackie,
Ex-Cornet Bruce Mactaggart, Bruce McCartney,
Allan McCredie, David Stewart, Ex-Cornet Charles N. Whillans.

Mmes. Wynn Alexander, Jeanette Brown, Aileen Douglas,
Margaret Mackay, Linda McCall, Sandra Riddell,
Elin Seeley, Maureen Smith, Linda Thompson.

Mss. Clare Button, Anne Cameron,
Lesley Fraser, Lynsey Fraser, Rachel Hosker.

Special thanks are due to J. Gordon Macdonald for the loan of books and documents, for his diligence in surveying the text and for his ever-generous and enthusiastic encouragement; to Professor Douglas Scott for his helpful pointers and suggestions; to Iain H. Scott, President of Hawick Archaeological Society, for his dynamism in driving forward this publication; to Hawick Common-Riding Committee for its continued interest in, and stewardship of, the Hawick songs and their history; and lastly, to my wife, Alison, for her endless patience and never-faltering support.

IWS

CONTENTS

ENTRIES

1. And We Ride
2. Anvil Crew, The
3. Auld Hawick, Ma Border Hame
4. Auld Hawick, My Dreams
5. Auld Hawick, Where I Was Born
6. Balbirnie, Arthur
7. Ballantyne, John ('Soapy')
8. Banner Blue, The
9. Best O' A', The
10. Bonnie Banner Blue, The
11. Bonnie Teviotdale
12. Border Queen, The
13. Borthwick Water
14. Brydon, Alan G.
15. Budge, Albert V.
16. Caldwell, Thomas
17. Callant's Song
18. Clinty's Song
19. Colledge, Adam N. McL.
20. Colour, The
21. Davidson, George
22. Douglas, Henry S.
23. Drumlanrig School Pupils
24. Dumbreck, Euphemia
25. Easton, William
26. Exile's Dream, The
27. Fairbairn, John
28. Fairest Spot O' A', The
29. Finnie, David
30. Gibb, David S.
31. Goodfellow, George L.
32. Gotterson, Matthew

33. Grant, Adam
34. Grant, Adam R.
35. Halliday, John
36. Hartop, Kerr
37. Hawick
38. Hawick Among The Hills
39. Hawick Callant, The
40. Hawick Lasses 1514
41. Hawick Reivers
42. Hawick Stands Alone
43. Hawick Volunteers
44. Hercus, James L.
45. Hogg, Frank
46. Hogg, James
47. Home By Burnfoot
48. Hornshole
49. Huggan, John
50. Hunter, James Y.
51. Hunter, Robert
52. Hurrah For The Cornet
53. I Like Auld Hawick
54. I Like Auld Hawick The Best
55. Ingles, Adam L.
56. Inglis, John
57. Invocation
58. Johnston, David
59. Ker, Tom
60. Kinly Stick
61. Laidlaw, Robert
62. Landles, Ian W.
63. Landles, William
64. Lassie That Works In The Mill, The
65. Letham, James G. A.
66. Mackay, Neil

67. McCartney, Robert
68. Meda's Song
69. Mosstrooper's Song, The
70. Murray, John E. D. (JED)
71. My Borderland
72. My Teviot Valley
73. Old Mill Town
74. Old Song, The
75. Oor Ain Auld Toon
76. Oor Bonnie Border Toon
77. Pawkie Paiterson
78. Peden, Walter A.
79. Queen O' The Auld Scottish Border, The
80. Return From Hornshole
81. Robson, William Inglis
82. Rosenberg, M.
83. Rutherford, John
84. Scott, Francis G.
85. Scott, Iain H.
86. Seeley, Ian W.
87. Simpson, Frank
88. Smith, Janet
89. Song O' Hawick, A
90. Songs Of Teviotdale
91. Taylor, Joshua J. H.
92. Teribus
93. Teviotdale
94. Thomson, James
95. Up Wi' Auld Hawick
96. Up Wi' The Banner
97. Wail Of Flodden, The
98. We'll Follow Oor Cornet Roon'
99. Where Slitrig And Teviot Meet
100. Where Teviot Rins

THE SONGS,
AUTHORS AND COMPOSERS

1. And We Ride

This (in its original) two-part male chorus song for soli and chorus comes from the pen of Alan Brydon **(14)** in the musical play *A Reiver's Moon* (first presented in Hawick Town Hall to great local acclaim 17th-20th April, 2007) Simply conceived, the song consists of two eight-bar phrases without modulation and a somewhat repetitive, though effective, chorus based on the second eight-bar phrase. The words are treated strophically. The song has found remarkable currency as a solo, but it is as a chorus that it works best. Key: C Maj. Range: C-D♭.

2. Anvil Crew, The

One of two extant humorous songs by William Easton (1853-1877) **(25)** – see also *Kinly Stick* **(60)**. Since Easton died at the age of only 24, it seems fairly likely that the words of this ditty (and possibly the tune also) come from around 1870, but they could be of earlier origin as Robert Murray[1] informs us that Easton was writing in this style for the amusement of his friends while still at school. Adam Ingles **(55),** in his *Notes and Comments on the Songs of Hawick*[2] describes the tune as 'rubbishy' and attributes it to Adam Grant **(33)**, but there is every likelihood that the tune is also of Easton's making, with a simple accompaniment for piano provided by Grant at a later date. Indeed, when Grant published it as the first of *Three Humorous Hawick Songs* before the First World War it was *arranged* by M. Rosenberg **(82)** – Grant's pseudonym – so, clearly, he was not seeking any credit for its creation. Easton's *métier* is local personalities and their activities – in this case, a description of a piece of tomfoolery with a raft (the *Anvil*) on the River Teviot between Albert Bridge and what is now Teviot Health Centre. References to the 'Gas hoose bar' and Laidlaw's Cauld are now historical allusions, since both, together with the firm of Laidlaw's, are now long gone. The song has a certain 'novelty' popularity, usually at a certain stage in an evening's proceedings – there are so many better Hawick songs – but it crops up, nevertheless, with remarkable regularity. The first report we have of it at an official Hawick gathering was the occasion of the Hawick Callants' Club Dinner in the Tower Hotel (now Drumlanrig's Tower) on Friday, 24th March, 1905[3] when it was sung by Ex-Cornet W. Thomas Grieve, accompanied on the piano by Adam Grant. It was sung at the Colour Bussing of 1907 by William P. Gaylor. For the Millennium revival of J.E.D. Murray's **(69)** play *The Gutterbludes* in April, 2000, Ian Seeley **(86)**, its Musical Director, reworked the melody to fit a set of Murray's verses for which the original music had been lost (cf. *A Funny Fellow* in *The Gutterbludes*). A somewhat ironic, if tragic, postscript to this song's history is evidenced in a report in *Hawick Express and Advertiser* 13/12/1918 of the death by drowning of Richard Newall (1850-1918) – the original 'boatswain Newall[4], who was up aloft' in the song. His body was found in the River Teviot where, so many years earlier, in the full exuberance of youth, he had cavorted with his fellow crew members on the *Anvil.* The tune is also alluded to in Seeley's overture to *The Gutterbludes.* Key: C Maj. Range: C-D♭.

3. Auld Hawick, Ma Border Hame

There can be few Hawick songs of the late 20th Century that have come to public recognition so quickly as has this song. The words and melody come from the pen of Ian W. Landles (b. 1952) **(62)**. Written during the 1996 summer of discontent when the infamous Lady Riders Dispute threatened to tear Hawick's Common Riding, indeed Hawick itself, apart, it was a timely reminder of the value of all the good things that make living in Hawick worthwhile. Most alarming at this time, perhaps, were the effects of a largely hostile and mischief-making media and it seemed as if all these favourable aspects of the town were to be cast aside in an argument which questioned ownership, exclusion and inclusion with regard to participation in the town's ancient ceremonies. This song, from one whose native love for the 'grey auld toon' is well documented, may be seen as an exhortation to take stock, be thankful and take pride and pleasure in what Hawick has to offer – '*So come, and A will show ti ee the spot that means the world tae me...*' The success of the song lies in its total lack of complexity. It doesn't seek to be smart in any way and is unashamedly a community song, and a good one to boot. It follows a well-tried formula; a strong melodic line is developed largely by means of modified repetition in both verse and chorus; and the subject material is clearly presented and not cluttered with an ornate accompaniment. From the standpoint of both soloist and chorus it sings well, and a rousing chorus invariably makes for a good Hawick song. The song was dedicated to Iain H. Scott **(85)** of 'Scocha' renown. The accompaniment is by Ian W. Seeley. **(86)** Key: C Maj. Range: $G_|$-$D^|$.

4. Auld Hawick, My Dreams

This attractive setting by Adam L. Ingles **(55)** of two verses of a longer poem by Robert H. Laidlaw (1872-1953) **(61)** never fails to take a trick at a Hawick Night, but so often it is emasculated by being sung too slowly, so failing to allow for the subtle changes in tempo which enrich a waltz song. The song need not be fast, but it requires to flow, however gently. Ingles's innate modesty inhibits him from calling it anything more than an *arrangement* and he states that 'The tune is anything but original as it bears a strong resemblance to many songs'[5]. That statement could be applied to many compositions and to many composers, both famous and obscure. If it does bear a passing resemblance to the German folksong *Die Lorelei* then it parallels a fine model, but we can safely assume that this is Ingles's work. The song dates

7

from the mid-1950s when it was written for Misses Jean Armstrong and Jeanette Johnston, both members of his choir when he was organist at Wilton South Church. Laidlaw's poem appeared in the *Hawick Express* of 13th June,1951. Key E♭ Maj. Range: Soprano – E♭-F[I], Contralto – C-D[I].

5. Auld Hawick, Where I Was Born

Another piece of self deprecation from Adam Ingles **(55)**; not, of course an *arrangement*, but his very own setting, albeit with similarities to whatever known melody the listener wishes to identify. (The Irish national anthem, as sung at rugby internationals, must be a contender for the last phrase). But that is neither here nor there. It remains a very fine setting of words originated by George Davidson (1846-1923) **(21)**. That is to say, the original words have been altered considerably by Ingles for his purpose. Davidson's original had three verses and Ingles has based his selection of words on the first and last verses. But, in truth, only the first line of the original last verse remains unaltered. The first verse has suffered somewhat less depredation. An earlier setting by one A. Jardine is extant in manuscript, but, while it follows Davidson's text to the letter, the music is considerably inferior to what Ingles has left us. In fairness to Adam Ingles, the sheet music he published for this song in 1950 does indicate 'Words *adapted* from a Poem by George Davidson'. On the same sheet he describes the music as being 'based on an Old Scottish Air' – a statement he amplifies in his *Notes and Comments on the Songs of Hawick* as *They're Aye A-Teasin' Me.* Musically, it should also be noted that what we have today is a vast improvement on the quasi-Victorian, ornate and clumsy accompaniment revealed in that publication in which semi-quaver arpeggios and ornaments abound. Ingles clearly felt a 'piano symphony' (taking a lead, perhaps, from Joshua J. H. Taylor's **(91)** setting of *The Banner Blue* **(8)**) at the end of the song would be appreciated so he ended with four bars of counterpoint based on *Teribus* **(93)** and Sir

Henry Bishop's *Home, Sweet Home.* For audiences today, alas, a song is considered to be at an end when the singer hits the final note. No doubt, by the time Ingles was editing *The Hawick Songs – A Complete Collection* between 1955 and 1957, he realised the changes that had taken place in public performance and a simpler conception of *Auld Hawick, Where I Was Born* was now required. His original was in the key of D♭ Major. He now dropped it by a semitone to C and ditched the semiquaver arpeggios, ornaments and the concluding symphony. The song made its debut at the Callants' Club Smoker for the Cornet on 5th May, 1950[6] when it was sung by James Kennedy, a railway blacksmith employed at the Lochpark Works, but one with a voice lauded by the great tenor, John Tainsh. Key: C Maj. Range: C-E♭.

6. Balbirnie, Arthur (b. 1735)

Arthur Balbirnie arrived in Hawick from Dunfermline in Fife during the latter part of the 18th Century to take up a position as foreman dyer in the carpet factory which operated in Orrock Place from *c.*1752 until its closure in 1806. (In all probability, he came on the recommendation of William Robertson (1720-1797), who also arrived from Dunfermline to set up the enterprise). Balbirnie was, however, a native of north east Fife, born at Kemback, and his christening was recorded at Dairsie on 6th April, 1735, his surname given as Balbirny. His fame in Hawick, however, rests upon his being the first Hawick song writer, to quote Robert Murray, 'of whom we have any note.'[7] His song, the 'founding song' so to speak, of the whole Hawick song writing tradition is, of course, '*The Old Song*' **(74)** to the *Air Eternal* (*Teribus*) **(92)**. Extant parish records reveal nothing of his passing or that of his daughter Katherine who, Robert Murray informs us, was married to one John Rae, needle maker. However, she is recorded, with her husband, in the census returns.

7. Ballantyne, John ('Soapy') (1803-1859)*

The Ballantyne family's musical contribution to Hawick's history can be traced from the middle of the 18th Century to the present day. John Ballantyne is something of a local legend. His prowess as a folk musician, fifer and fiddler has been much lauded and yet documentation with regard to his life is hard won. For a popular local worthy, it is remarkable that his passing should excite no comment from the local Press (although, admittedly, local journalism was in its infancy at this time). His real claim to local fame is that he is, today, credited with writing *Pawkie Paiterson* **(77)** and setting it to the tune we have today. But even this attribution has been contested. From the graveyard registry of St. Mary's we can conjecture the year of his birth – 1803, that he was a stocking maker and that he died at his home, 9 Kirk Wynd on 30th October, 1859 aged 56. But here, the sketchy information ends. Possibly he is the same John Ballantyne, stocking maker with William Laidlaw and Sons, who was recorded in the *Hawick (Monthly) Advertiser* (6/1/1855) as having donated 1/- to the Crimea War Fund. Related reports may assist in adding some flesh to his biography. For example, a paragraph devoted to his cousin, Walter Ballantyne ('Wat The Drummer'), in the *Hawick Advertiser* (4/6/1881) reveals that Wat, 59 years earlier, before he took to drumming, 'was one of the fifers, having for his first compeers such noted musicians as Caleb Rutherford and 'Soap' Ballantyne.' The period being described here is pre-1822, incidentally, the period of *The Old Song* **(74)**. The origin of the nickname 'Soapy' is lost. Hawick is a great place for nicknames and these are often carried through families, even unrelated families with the same surname. It is interesting, but frustrating therefore, to the researcher, that William Scott, writing in Hawick Archaeological Society's Transactions (April, 1890) on 'Auld Hawick', gives many local nicknames, but there is no mention of the legendary 'Soapy.' William Laidlaw of Cumledge Mills, Duns (b.

Hawick 1821) remembered seeing 'Soapy' 'walk from the Pant Well to the head of the Sandbed playing his fiddle, while two boys took a collection for his benefit.'[8] The stuff of legend, indeed.

*There is at least one other John Ballantyne contemporary with the above (aged 50 in the 1841 Census), with similar credentials, but born in Selkirk. He *could* be the one of that name who also died at Kirk Wynd, but in 1856. However, his recorded age at death (58 years) does not tally with the 1841 Census return. On the balance of probability, the writer has opted for the above but, ultimately, this is no more than informed conjecture.

8. Banner Blue, The

This triumphant yet reverential song was composed by a Yorkshire man, Joshua J. H. Taylor (1831-1910) **(91)** to words by John Inglis (1838-1928) **(56)** originally entitled *The Banner Of Blue.* The song appears to have been written in 1892, J.E.D. Murray**(70)** noting, that year, 'His (Inglis') new song, *The Banner of Blue,* now published for the first time, has not yet been weighed in the balances, but, doubtless, should the music specially composed for it be equal to the sentiment, it will not be found wanting.'[9] Its original Victorian accompaniment renders it a far more dramatic piece than the Ingles **(55)** edited version used today. This is a song written by a more musically erudite composer than Adam Grant **(33)** and it shows in the original piano part which, in some ways, presages the work of the cinema pianist before the advent of the 'talkies'. It is the single Hawick song in which the piano accompaniment appears to react to, or comment upon, the text, copious directions leaving the performers in no doubt as to the composer's intentions – *con furore, recitando* among them. The original is cleverly written with allusions to *Teribus* **(92)** cropping up in the accompaniment. It is also a song which requires a capable singer if it is to have its maximum impact. There is, however, another problem, which Ingles was attempting to address, namely finding a pianist capable of doing justice to Taylor. So what we have now is a compromise – a simple accompaniment with Taylor's melody more or less intact. Less, actually, because in spite of his promise in 1955 to Hawick Common Riding Committee (as the copyright holders) that the melodies would remain unaltered, Adam Ingles proved cavalier when he changed the last four bars of the last chorus which, in the original, were different from those of the previous choruses. An editor shoulders great responsibility in the transmission of the work of others. (see below). Taylor's original had a 10 bar introduction, 6 bar codetta and a 12 bar concluding 'symphony' 'for the Common Riding only'. The original key of the song was A♭ Major.

As can be seen above, Ingles opts for none of the composer's melodies, but gives his own instead.

He transposed the song into G Major, but, for melodic comparison, his melody is retained in A flat Major.

This was one of only four of our existing Hawick songs to be published by the celebrated local booksellers, W. & J. Kennedy of the Sandbed before the First World War (most were published by Adam Grant). The song's first performance at an official function was given by James Haig at the Colour Bussing ceremony of 1894. He gave a repeat performance at the 1895 ceremony and 1896 saw it taken up by Hawick's celebrated tenor, John Bell with Adam Grant **(33)** as accompanist. Key: G Maj. Range: D-E♭.

9. Best O' A', The

This song could pay dividends in proportion to the input required to pull it off. The words were written by Kerr Hartop (b.1996)**(36)** while he was a pupil at Hawick High School, and set to an easy going, if unadventurous, twelve bar melody by one of his teachers, James Letham.**(65)** It is one of only three Hawick songs to be written in compound (6/8) time (the others being *Hawick Stands Alone* **(42)** and *Pawkie Paiterson* **(77)**). The composer, to relieve repetitiousness, has set the last verse a tone higher than the starting key and this gives the song a bit more musical interest. The song was written for 'The Big Sing' (2011) at Mansfield Park, Hawick, when it was sung by the massed voices of local primary schools and the early years of Hawick High School. It has been performed very acceptably by Wilton Primary School Choir, but is in need of a champion to popularise it. Key: E♭/F Maj. Range: B♭♭- D♭.

10. Bonnie Banner Blue, The

With words and music by Alan G. Brydon (b. 1961) **(14)** this song is surely one of the triumphs of the renascence which Hawick song, as a particular genre, has undergone since around the mid-1980s. It embraces almost every commendable attribute of the highly successful late Victorian and Edwardian Hawick classics – relevant, evocative words, a strong, easily remembered melodic line and a passionate chorus. It is, though, in some ways, a 'one off' in its almost hypnotic quality. It 'claims' the listener, who will almost inevitably find the melody swimming in his head after a first hearing. It sounds simultaneously of several influences (Scottish traditional song, folk rock, popular 'anthem') and none. Unfortunately, it is one of a number of fine new Hawick songs that appeared too late for inclusion in the 2001 revised and extended edition of *The Hawick Songs – A Complete Collection (ed. Seeley)*[10] published by Hawick Callants' Club, but there can be no doubt that its place in any subsequent revision is assured. It is a song that requires no champion. Many different singers perform it. It stands on its undeniable worth and quality. The song made its first public impact at the Annual Dinner of the Ancient Order of Mosstroopers on 27th May, 2005 in Hawick Town Hall when it was sung by Iain H. Scott **(85)** in the presence of the composer, who was one of the guest speakers on that occasion. The published piano accompaniment was devised by Iain H. Scott **(85)** and realised by Ian W. Seeley **(86)**. The ornamentation in the accompaniment, reminiscent of 'dirls' in Scottish folk music, renders it something of a teaser for the pianist, calling for some deft fingerwork. Key: A Maj. Range: $A_|$-$D^|$.

11. Bonnie Teviotdale

The words and melody of this engagingly simple yet attractive love song are by John Halliday (1821-1902) **(35)**. Not one word is wasted and Halliday succeeds in conveying his love for his native Teviotdale, its people and his own personal belovèd without recourse to dripping sentimentality. With regard to the melody, musically, one feels that the first eight bars sound more like an ending than a beginning, but this in no way detracts from its overall beauty. If anything does diminish this gem, it is a feature which has crept in over recent years whereby singers, in the final verse, supplant the simple charm of the last two bars with an 'Andy Stewart'[11] ending (see following page) in the mistaken belief that this, in some way, enhances the song and their performance of it (more the latter). Far from it; it cheapens the song musically and as such is to be deprecated. This beautiful song requires no such embellishment and is damaged by it.

Last phrase - all verses

For her dear sake I'll nev-er leave Oor Bon-nie Tev-iot-dale.

Bastardised last phrase - last verse

For her dear sake I'll nev-er leave Oor Bon-nie Tev-iot-dale

The song was in circulation for many years before Adam Grant **(33)** published his arrangement of it in 1924, dedicating it to the memory of Andrew Rutherford Oliver of Thornwood (now Mansfield House Hotel), Hawick. Indeed, the *Hawick Advertiser* (2/1/1875) reports Oliver singing this 'new song' at Richardson, Noble & Co.'s Factory Soiree & Ball in the Masonic Hall on Old Year's Night, 1874, describing 'This original song by a local aspirant to poetical fame...when we say that the air is well adapted to the words, we give it no faint praise.' The key then was D Major. It is the only song to have been put *up* a key by Adam Ingles **(55)** in the 1957 edition of *The Hawick Songs – A Complete Collection*[12] (most of the others came down). The most recent arrangement of the song is that by Ian Seeley **(86)** in the 2001 edition of the collection. *Bonnie Teviotdale* has consistently maintained its popularity among all age groups of performers. Key: E♭ Maj. Range: D-E♭[1].

12. Border Queen, The

If there is a 'top three' for Hawick songs, this one, with music by John Rutherford (1838-1914) **(83)** to James Thomson's (1827-1888) **(94)** words must surely vie with *Up Wi' The Banner* **(96)** (words again by Thomson) for second place (no-one will deny *Teribus* **(92)** first!). These two songs are unsurpassed as marches which, when played by Hawick Saxhorn Band, provide a magnificent accompaniment to the procession and cavalcade as it passes through the town's High

Street on Common Riding Friday. The words of *The Border Queen* (which appear in the 1884 reprint and enlargement of Thomson's *Doric Lays And Lyrics*) extol Hawick and the advantages her people enjoy while affecting pity for the other Border towns, particularly Galashiels, for not being so fortunate – all banter and good humour underpinned by a truly memorable melody. The four bar introduction is based on the opening phrase of *Teribus* **(92)**. Here again, Adam Ingles **(55)**, besides altering the original accompaniment, has altered Rutherford's melody by one note and one rhythm at bars 17 and 18 (see following page). Only one note and a rhythm, but it is of great significance because the Ingles version is now taken as gospel by the overwhelming majority of singers (more about this in entry **97**) and Ian Seeley **(86)**, as editor in 2001, has retained this on the basis of wont and usage. Hawick Saxhorn Band continues to play the authentic version in Robert Rimmer's (1863-1934)[13] medley arrangement – *Hawick Songs* (c.1913).The original key was G Major. The melody is at least a year or two older than that of Inglis Robson for *Up Wi' The Banner* **(96)**. The question is – did Rutherford write the melody before his emigration to Australia in 1884, or later? (he made return visits to Hawick in 1892 and 1901 but these dates are too late for the song's reported appearance). The Rutherford tune was definitely in print in 1892 (James Edgar advertised it on the back cover of his *Songs and Recitations*). Adam Ingles **(55)** dates the song around 1880[14], but the present writer believes this to be five or six years too early. Unusually, for a 'new Hawick song' in this period, it does not appear to have received any prior publicity in the local press, even though it was published by Adam Grant **(33)**, nor did it appear to excite any comment following its first reported public performance by Ex-Cornet Scott Irvine at the Colour Bussing of 1887. Inglis Robson's setting of *Up Wi' The Banner* was published the following year, 1888. Key: F Maj. Range: C-D].

Rutherford's original

What though her lads are wild a - wee

Ingles 1957 alteration

What tho' her lads are wild a - wee

13. Borthwick Water

This song is one of a number that Adam Ingles (1914-1991) **(55)** sketched out in manuscript after the 1957 Hawick song collection was published. Unfortunately, it had to lie among his papers for a decade after his death before the opportunity arose to have it published. The arrangement in the 2001 collection is by its musical editor, Ian W. Seeley **(86)**. The words, by William Landles (1912-1998) **(63)** first appeared in the Edinburgh *Evening News* (26/4/1935) and were reprinted in the *Hawick Express* of 25th May, 1935. The words are perhaps rendered bland by the 3/4 melody, so compromising the song's impact. The reverse of this process is seen to advantage in *Auld Hawick, My Dreams* **(4)** in which Ingles had the good sense to omit Laidlaw's **(61)** verse about the Cornet riding with his men. Such words could have appeared incongruous with the saccharine harmonies and waltz time of that song. Nevertheless, *Borthwick Water* is a pleasing song that could repay investment, but, like all new or unfamiliar songs, it needs a selfless champion to keep it before the public. There are notable examples of this happening and transforming a song's fortunes. *The Fairest Spot O' A'* **(28)** is one such. The problem is that most singers are not selfless and opt for 'their' song or the song that affords them perceived *cachet* at the expense of songs such as this. *Borthwick Water* has been performed at the 1514 Club's 'Hawick Sings' annual concerts from their earliest days and was sung in duet form by Alison Seeley and Etta

McKean, two High School teachers, at the 1514 concert in Hawick Old Parish Church Hall on 20th May, 1987. It is sung occasionally by its author's son, Ian W. Landles **(62)**. Key: G Maj. Range: D-D¹.

14. Brydon, Alan G.

Born in Hawick on 10th February, 1961, Alan Gilbert Brydon represents something of the culture of enterprise that the town's beleaguered knitwear industry needs in the face of seemingly relentless retrenchment and recession. Having attended Hawick High School, he entered the time-honoured industry, qualifying as a carding engineer at the Scottish College of Textiles, Galashiels. His developing expertise in the technology of knitwear saw him become the author of various publications in the field and embark on a career of consultation, development and lecturing combined with his own technology-based interests in the industry, which was to see him accept a visiting professorship at Leeds University, take him all over the world and sharpen his appreciation of his home town. His passion for the town and its history is insatiable. His historical novel, *The Keeper of Teviotdale* reveals an intimate knowledge of his provenance and he has found a mentor and collaborator in local historian Ian W. Landles **(62)** with whom he wrote the outstandingly successful local musical *A Reiver's Moon* in 2007. He has proved to be a prolific local song writer whose work is highly popular, songs such as *Auld Jock* and *Man O' Mony Pairts* among them. His songs for the much acclaimed Hawick folk rock band 'Scocha', of which he was a member for several years (singing, playing guitar and pipes), are no less beguiling. His evocative *Callin' Doon The Line* and patriotic *Scotland's Calling* bespeak a wide ranging creative ability. His Hawick-specific songs have been dominated by the outstanding success of his *The Bonnie Banner Blue* **(10).** His *Return From Hornshole* **(80)** is worthy of a wider audience. A gifted after-dinner speaker, Alan Brydon was the chosen Principal Guest at the 2010 Common Riding and he did not disappoint, his speech being delivered in rhyme. A keen horseman, he was president of the Ancient Order of Mosstroopers in 2012.

15. Budge, Albert V. (1901-1967)

The composer of *My Borderland* **(71)**, Albert Victor Budge, was born at 3 Morrison Place, Hawick on 2nd February, 1901 – son of George Budge, printer. He was employed in the knitwear industry by the firm of Innes, Henderson and Co. (later Braemar, and eventually subsumed in Pringle of Scotland), but had an avid interest in music whetted by organ lessons from David B. Simpson, FRCO,[15] the distinguished organist of St. George's Church. Outwith his day job, he was variously church organist, conductor and composer. He was appointed organist of St. Margaret's, Wilton (where Langlands Court now stands) at the end of 1930 and he was conductor of the Braemar Choir in the years immediately following the Second World War. He had an enjoyable association with Hawick PSA Male Voice Choir, becoming its deputy conductor in 1948 and conductor in 1949. The song for which he is remembered was written in 1950 to words by David Johnston (1900-1982) **(58)**. The last years of Budge's life were spent at 1 Ettrick Terrace. He died suddenly at Hawick Cottage Hospital on 5th June, 1967 at the age of 66 and is buried in Wellogate Cemetery.

16. Caldwell, Thomas (1854-1915)

Born in Galashiels on 7th November, 1854 of Irish parentage (his father was a cloth broker) but reared in Hawick at 6 Kirk Wynd, Thomas Caldwell was to become one of Hawick's most renowned speakers of the late–Victorian and Edwardian periods. He was one of a group of minor but significant *literati* and *cognoscenti* which Hawick was fortunate to be able to claim. The Victorian growth of Hawick and the completion of a through railway between Edinburgh and the English cities in 1862 accelerated a healthy thirst for learning and the performing arts. Artistes, lecturers and all manner of nationally acclaimed personalities could now be heard at Hawick's Exchange Hall (Professor Blackie, for example, on 'The Love Songs of Scotland' – 24th February, 1890). Hawick Archaeological Society had been founded in 1856, Hawick Choral Union in 1860 and, of course, there was Hawick Literary Society which would have more than a passing influence on the writing of Hawick songs (see e.g. *I Like Auld Hawick* **(53)**). Caldwell, Ker **(59),** Inglis, **(56)** and Murray **(70)** were all beneficiaries of this new age of self-improvement. Caldwell started out training as a pupil teacher at Drumlanrig School with the intention of becoming a teacher but had to abandon his ambition on the death of his father. Following a period of employment in local mills, he operated in the stationery and newspaper trade (itself a Victorian success story). Always interested in politics and being an avid Liberal supporter, he developed his skill in oratory through his involvement with the East Bank Literary Society, of which he was a prominent member. Fearless in debate and quite at ease courting controversy, he was ever a generous opponent. He came to prominence locally in the Irish Home Rule debate of 1886 when he switched his allegiance from George Trevelyan to A. L. Brown because he believed a Liberal principle to be threatened. His party loyalty was recognised and, in 1893, he left Hawick to live in Edinburgh on his appointment as an organiser on the staff of the Scottish Liberal Association, but it was in literary matters that he found greatest satisfaction and it was for such that he was held in high esteem by his fellow townsfolk. It was Caldwell who was largely instrumental in having the James Thomson **(94)** Memorial erected in Wellogate Cemetery and it was he who unveiled it on 3rd June, 1899. During the 1890s and 1900s Caldwell gave highly acclaimed musically illustrated lectures in collaboration with the renowned Hawick tenor John Bell, to whom, in 1902, he and Adam

Grant **(33)** dedicated *Up Wi' Auld Hawick* **(95).** His other memorable collaboration with Grant is, of course, *Oor Ain Auld Toon* **(75)**. We read that his lecture – 'Burns As A Songwriter', for example, enthralled the audience at London Road U.F. Church in Edinburgh on 16th March, 1907. He was a founder member of both Hawick Liberal Club and Hawick Callants' Club in addition to being a prominent member of the Edinburgh Borderers' Union. He was ever a popular choice for giving a toast at the functions of all three associations and his presence at the annual 'Hawick Night' of the latter was a highlight in their calendar. His Masonic connection was with Lodge St. James 424. Caldwell died suddenly, aged 60, at 17 Royal Park Terrace, Edinburgh on 3rd July, 1915 and was buried in Wellogate Cemetery, Hawick.

17. Callant's Song

This vigorous song was the eventual result of a word-setting exercise given to Higher Music Examination candidates when Ian Seeley **(86)** was Head of Music at Hawick High School. Only the first verse was given to pupils. On completion of the exercise the results were considered, after which the teacher gave an exemplar. Basically, this was it, and it was duly filed. On the recommendation of its president, Ronnie Nichol, the 1514 Club invited Seeley to speak at their Annual Dinner on 3rd June, 1994 in Drumlanrig School. The composer decided that it would be a fitting gesture to dedicate and present a new Hawick song to Nichol to honour his presidency, so he resurrected the exercise and added two more verses (all the words were his own in order to avoid copyright restrictions). His friend, local Salvation Army Corps Bandmaster J. Elliot Renwick, at that time a director of Buccleuch Printers, printed and published the song, which was sold at the dinner for the benefit of the Club's projects. It was sung by the noted Hawick tenor Elliot Goldie on that occasion with the composer at the piano. This was, in fact, to be the first of five

Hawick songs written by Seeley between 1994 and 1996. The musical style owes much to the 'school song' genre and is reminiscent of the songs of the English composer Thomas F. Dunhill (1877-1946). It has a strong melodic line which makes characteristic allusions to *Teribus* **(92).** The words draw heavily on sentiments expressed in Hawick Callants' Club constitution. Key: G Maj. Range: D-E$^|$.

18. Clinty's Song

This is one of the two extant original songs from the Edwardian melodrama of 1905/06, *The Gutterbludes*, by J.E.D. Murray (1858-1936) **(70)** (the other being *Meda's Song* **(68)**). The incidental music for the play, which was produced at the Exchange over four nights (30th December, 1905, 1st-3rd January, 1906), was composed by Murray's friend and contemporary, Adam Grant (1859-1938) **(33)**. 'Clinty' was the nickname of Robert Oliver (1772-1847), tailor and town councillor of Hawick, the name being derived from his paternal home 'Clinthead' which stood at the Silver Street end of the Auld Brig. Why he is even in the play at all is a mystery (and a headache for any producer) for his character contributes absolutely nothing to the plot. It seems as if Murray contrived a kind of 'guest appearance' for Mr. William Turnbull who was something of a local celebrity in the field of stage monologues. This, however, is no monologue, but a rather fine serious song. In fact, it shows Adam Grant, arguably, at his best in the hymn tune-like chordal style of accompaniment with which he was most comfortable. The mood of the song is austere and philosophical and it benefits greatly from being performed by a rich bass voice. Certainly, the opening introductory unison octave bars juxtaposed with a chordal cadence in the piano part are commanding and the sense of contemplation is enhanced by judiciously placed pauses. Turnbull sang the song at the Colour Bussing of 1908 and Grant published the sheet music for the song at the end of that year, the *Hawick*

Advertiser describing it as 'sung by Mr. W. Turnbull, of whom a photo in character is given... and lovers of local music will be glad to add this quaintly worded song to their repertoire.'[16] (The cost was 1/-). Key: G Maj. Range: B⌐-D⌐.

19. Colledge, Adam Norman McLeod (1872-1965)

It is fitting that this professional musician should be remembered as the composer of *The Mosstrooper's Song* **(69)** because, music apart, his great passion in life was horses. He had savoured the joy of the gallop in the Border hills but, like every horseman, he knew that there was no shame in literally coming down to earth. He had 'kissed the gress!' An entry in the Log Book of Hawick High School (13/5/1929) informs us of his absence, 'suffering from a fractured breast bone as the result of a fall from a horse.' He was a frequent supporter of the Buccleuch Hunt, a mounted supporter at Hawick and Selkirk Common Ridings and a member of the Ancient Order of Mosstroopers. His son, Tom, was Acting Father at Hawick Common Riding in 1953. Adam Colledge was born at Summershall House, Edinburgh on 16th June, 1872, the son of a draper and great-grandson of a Denholm stockingmaker. On the early death of his father, his mother brought her young family of thirteen to Selkirk to raise them. Adam became a solicitor's clerk, firstly in Selkirk, then in Lamlash, Arran, where he became organist in the parish church. Returning to Selkirk, he became organist of the Episcopal Church. This was followed by a spell at Walkerburn Parish Church during which time he continued his musical studies at St. Mary's Cathedral, Edinburgh under Dr. Tom Collinson, gaining the ALCM diploma. In May, 1901, he succeeded the Swiss-born Dr. K. E. Reinle[17] as organist of Hawick Old Parish Church (Frank Scott Court now occupies its site) and set up as a music teacher at 6 Dakers Place. In 1903, having upgraded his qualifications to LLCM, he became a part time music and singing teacher in Hawick schools. By 1907, according to Hawick High School Log Book, he appears to have received a full-time appointment in that school, a post he retained until his retirement on 14th July, 1937. Colledge, prior to his retirement, lived at 6 Douglas Road, but on that event moved to 'The Poplars', Denholm. He died at Edinburgh Royal Infirmary on 22nd May, 1965 in his 93rd year and was interred in Shawfield Cemetery, Selkirk.

20. Colour, The

This is the original title given by James Hogg (1780-1838) **(46)** to the verses we use today as the Common Riding Song proper, i.e. *Teribus* **(92)**. Published in 1819, it quickly superseded Balbirnie's **(6)** *Old Song* **(74)** as the Common Riding 'anthem'. Technically speaking, then, *Teribus* is the tune. The slogan, or rallying cry, 'Teribus', is incorporated in Hogg's chorus (as with Balbirne's) as 'Teribus ye Teriodin' – a supposed invocation to the mythological Scandinavian gods Thor and Odin – TYR HAEB US YE TYR, YE ODIN, as the decorative balcony banner of Hawick Town Hall proclaims at the Common Riding. Thor was the god of thunder and Odin, his father, the chief god – the 'All-wise'. The Norse connection sometimes elicits surprise, but the Angles who colonised Northumbria (or Bernicia, as it was known) in the 5th Century came from the southern part of the Jutland peninsula which fell under Scandinavian influence. Further to this, the Viking raiders of the 7th and 8th centuries left their footprints all over Northumbria, Cumbria and southern Scotland. We need only look to the village of Torthorwald, near Dumfries, for further evidence of this influence. This is one theory, promoted by Sir James Murray of Oxford English Dictionary renown, but it is damaged by the lack of a convincing explanation for the presence of 'Odin' in the slogan. Another is that the 'Tyr' is indeed Tyr – the god of war in a different Teutonic Pantheon. A further strand in the etymology is in early British (basically Welsh and related Celtic languages, excluding Gaelic) which sees it as a corruption of Tyr y Bas (place/land of flatness/calm/

serenity?!). None of this should be taken to imply that our Border ancestors worshipped such gods; this is about the origin of the word 'Teribus.' It should also be noted that the 'Odin' part seems to have arrived only with Balbirnie **(6)** and Hogg **(46)** as they sought rhyming couplets for 'common' and 'Flodden' respectively. 'Wont and usage' has done the rest. All the indications, however, are that the Hawick tune originated in Northumbria (the border of which is a mere twelve miles from Hawick), and it is a very different tune to that bearing the same name, played by pipe bands in other parts of the country (see also entry **92**). Adam Ingles **(55)**, in his *Notes And Comments On The Songs Of Hawick*, highlights the flaws in the historical account as related in Hogg's verses. The problem is similar to that which besets the William Wallace story. The boundaries between fact and folk legend have become blurred through lack of surviving records or through embellishment as a result of wishful thinking. There can be no doubt that a heroic act occurred in 1514 at, or near, Hornshole, outside Hawick, but the details of the scenario as presented by Hogg will not stand up fully against historical deduction. Hawick's late Honorary Provost, Frank Scott, would not have Druids at any price! All this said, Hogg's is an inspiring interpretation accommodating what is definitely known. One or two alterations have been made since Hogg revised and corrected his poem for publication by J. D. Kennedy in 1837. His original verse 1 was '... *a Druid's dark prediction...*' (now verse 20); his original verse 2 - '*Scotia felt thine ire...*' is now verse 1; and two verses have been added – a new verse 2 – '*Sacred was the widow's portion*' and, to suit the ceremonial role of the Cornet's Acting Father, at verse 19 – '*Magistrates! Be faithful trustees...*' Who says tradition dictates an unchangeable order? In 1892, verse 2 was '... *Drumlanrig, generous donor...*' This demonstrates that the Hawick tradition, though essentially remaining constant, is ever under review. The song was originally printed in Kelso, the Hawick printer having rejected it owing to the inclusion of some satirical verses which were later abandoned. It was first sung at the Common Riding of 1819 by a former apprentice of Hogg, one James Scott. The melody and its rhythm is subject to variation depending upon where it is heard. The version played by Hawick Drum and Fife Band is different to the sung version though very recognisably the same *Teribus*. The musical form is binary – an eight bar verse followed by an eight bar chorus containing a curious 'modal' shift after two bars, giving a general key orientation of Lydian mode transposed. Key: G Maj. Range: F-D^l.

21. Davidson, George (1846-1923)

George Davidson, the originator of the words for *Auld Hawick, Where I Was Born* (5) was born in Hawick on 22nd December, 1846. Although a plasterer to trade, he developed a flair for writing poetry, some of which occasionally appeared in the *Hawick Express*. He eventually became Bard to Masonic Lodge St. John No. 111 of which he was a dedicated member and at which he recited and sang his own pieces. He died, aged 76, at 24 Bridge Street, Hawick on 30th June, 1923 and was buried in Wellogate Cemetery.

22. Douglas, Henry S. (b. 1935)

There can be few more kenspeckle figures in Hawick and its environs than Henry Scott Douglas – farmer, churchman, folk singer and Common Riding stalwart. He is, as his surname indicates, a Borderer through and through. Born of farming stock at Catslackburn in the Yarrow valley on 9th August, 1935, he attended Yarrow and Philiphaugh Schools. On his father moving to Craik in 1946, he attended Hawick High School. The Douglas family made a further move to Hyndlee and finally, in 1949, to Howahill, some three miles south of Hawick, where Henry has farmed for the past fifty years on his own account. He was Acting Father to Cornet Derek Inglis in 1978 and is one of very few who have held the presidency of the three Common Riding-affiliated clubs

– the 1514 Club in 1983; the Ancient Order of Mosstroopers in 1989; and Hawick Callants' Club in 2008. He proved to be a very effective chairman of the Callants' Club sub-committee appointed in 2000 to bring the 2001 edition of *The Hawick Songs – A Complete Collection* to fruition. He was also Official Song Singer to Hawick Common Riding 1985-2000. His passion for folk singing has taken him to venues all over Scotland and he has rubbed shoulders with the most distinguished exponents of the genre. His love of Burns songs is revealed each January when he is often the indispensable choice of artiste for the celebration of the Bard. Ever a favourite for his Common Riding renditions, he has championed Walter Peden's **(78)** *The Lassie That Works In The Mill* **(64)**, one of the 'new' entries in the 2001 Hawick collection and a song entirely suited to Douglas's folk singing expertise.

23. Drumlanrig School Pupils

The encouragement of schoolchildren in Hawick to embrace the culture and spirit of the Common Riding is well established and reinforced by the efforts of the 1514 Club. Poetry, essay and art competitions are of the essence so it should be no surprise to find a class of pupils at Drumlanrig St. Cuthbert's Primary School in 1968 creating a poem, *Hurrah! For The Cornet* **(52)** which their teacher, Mrs. Janet Smith **(88)** set to music. The school choir has given performances of it in recent years at the 1514 Club's 'Hawick Sings' concerts.

24. Dumbreck, Euphemia (1810-1879)

Mrs. Dumbreck's name in Hawick will forever be associated with the beautiful melody she provided for Frank Hogg's **(45)** poem *I Like Auld Hawick* **(53)**. She was born Euphemia Kinnear, of farming stock, at Fingask, Rhynd (some five miles south-east of Perth) on 27th October, 1810 and married John Dumbreck on 7th November, 1830. She arrived in Hawick in May, 1865 with her husband and daughters

Euphemia[18] and Katherine from Woodhall Bank, Juniper Green, Edinburgh to set up a boarding and day school for young ladies in 'that CORNER NEW HOUSE at the foot of NORTH BRIDGE STREET'.[19] English, French, German, Italian, Music, Singing, Drawing and Painting were taught, so it was a centre of cultural aspiration. Her husband died the following year, but the school, which she named Teviotside House (now 1 Teviotside Terrace – a guest house), would run until 1885 when her daughters retired to Colinton, Edinburgh. Euphemia Dumbreck died at the District Asylum, Melrose on 23rd November, 1879, having suffered from 'melancholia' (dementia). Her last resting place is St. Cuthbert's churchyard at the West end of Princes Street, Edinburgh.

25. Easton, William S. (1853-1877)

The author of *The Anvil Crew* (2) and *Kinly Stick* (60) was born at 1 High Street, Hawick in 1853, the son of hairdresser George Easton. William Scott Easton, a journeyman millwright, was employed by the Hawick Gas Company but in his leisure time he developed a *penchant* for writing humorous verse, revealed while he was still a schoolboy, and though virtually all of his other work is lost, Robert Murray ascribes to him the promise of greater, more serious work had he lived longer. Murray gives a very fine example of this in a piece found in Easton's private notebook after his death. The poem is *Alane*,[20] in which Easton laments lost love (through death). Though he became Bard of Masonic Lodge St. John 111, Easton did not live to fulfil that promise. A keen Volunteer, he was accidentally shot dead after standing in for an absent fellow soldier as a marker in target practice at Whitlaw Range, Hummelknows on 10th August, 1877. His grave is in Wellogate Cemetery. He was in his 24th year.

26. Exile's Dream, The

We first hear of this song from a report in the *Hawick Express* of 15th December, 1932 where it is described as 'A New Hawick Song.' It was subsequently advertised in the following week's edition describing 'Quantities available from the Author, Mr. John Fairbairn, 8 Union Street, Hawick. Terms on application.' An auspicious launching then, but this song has struggled for widespread recognition in spite of its being embraced by one or two respected locals, among them Mr. James Anderson and Mrs. Anne McMichan. The sheet music was still being sold by John Graham, newsagent of the Sandbed, until his death in 1974, and it continued to be sung by the faithful, though, it has to be said, with some deviation from the original, particularly in the rhythm of the chorus. In the year of its publication, John Fairbairn **(27)** was 74 years of age and the composer, John Huggan **(49)** 18. True, the composer had a bit to learn about harmony and arrangement, but the song has, nevertheless, a stirring melody suited to the sentiment of the words and it would make a fine band march. It deserves a higher public profile than it has achieved hitherto. The song should have been included in the 1957 Hawick song collection, but when Adam Ingles **(55)** approached the composer for permission to do so, his request was declined. John Huggan was, at that time, Head of Music in Galashiels Academy and was diffident about having what he considered immature work further exposed, nor did he show any inclination to revise it. Its inclusion in the 2001 edition of the song anthology was facilitated by permission being granted by the overall copyright holder, John Fairbairn's niece, Agnes. This enabled the editor to make some minor enhancements to the piano part. The song consists of two eight bar sections with a simple modulation from the home key to the dominant (D Major), which leads into a stirring chorus. In 2009 an attempt to bastardise the song by perpetuating the errors which had crept into the melody was frustrated by the threat of legal action by Huggan's daughter, Dr. Elizabeth Currie, supported by the musical editor of the anthology. The song in its unadulterated form awaits a champion who will give it the performance and the respect that it deserves. Key: G Maj. Range: C#-D♭.

27. Fairbairn, John (1858-1943)

A son of the village blacksmith, John Fairbairn was born at Maxton, Roxburghshire on 3rd August, 1858. He came to Hawick in the early 1900s and eventually became manager of the King's Theatre (the first nominal reincarnation of the Exchange; it would much later become the Marina and finally, Bogarts, before being gutted by fire; the remaining part of the Exchange is now Hawick Heritage Hub). He retired in 1928. Of a literary bent, he produced verses on various subjects, many for private circulation, and the occasional piece found publication in the *Hawick Express* over some forty years – poems such as *Alec, Oor Bellman, On Seeing A Tramp Passing, Look On The Bright, The Cornet's Chase, Wilton Park,* etc. His *The Exile's Dream* **(26)** with John Huggan **(49)** as composer will ensure his memory in Hawick. He expressed the hope in 1932 that 'it would form an acceptable gift to callants at home or in distant parts.' Fairbairn was a kenspeckle figure in the town, enjoying robust health until the day of his death – which occurred suddenly, when he was 85 years of age, in his home at 25 Wilton Crescent on 28th November, 1943. His remains are interred in Wellogate Cemetery.

28. Fairest Spot O' A', The

For thirty years before the Second World War this song virtually disappeared and was all but forgotten, having had its last concert airing when Mr. A. Caldwell sang it at the Colour Bussing of 1909 with Adam Grant at the piano. It does not appear to have been in print at that time and there is no evidence to suggest that Adam Grant **(33)** ever considered publishing it. The words and melody are by Tom Ker **(59)**. Grant had previously arranged and published Ker's very successful *I Like Auld Hawick The Best* **(54)** but he clearly did not feel the inclination to set Ker's other two songs (now published in the 2001 revision of the Hawick song anthology). The *Hawick Express* (25/5/1949) avers that the song's revival (along with *Where Slitrig And Teviot Meet* **(99)**) was 'made possible by some notes left by Tom Ker and Adam Grant and memorised by Adam R. Grant **(34)**, who has arranged them.' Apparently, both songs had been popular at functions held by the old Teviotdale Amateur Bicycle Club (of which Adam Grant senior was captain) around 1890. The relaunching of *The Fairest Spot O'A'* took place at Hawick Callants' Club's Congratulatory Smoker for Cornet Charles N. Whillans on 14th May, 1948 when it was sung by Mr. George. L. MacDonald (Cornet William Mactaggart's Acting Father in 1930 and a traveller for Innes, Henderson & Co.). It is a quietly passionate song whose rating, if not popularity, has risen gradually over the years since, undoubtedly assisted by its inclusion in the 1957 *The Hawick Songs – A Complete Collection* (*arranged Adam L. Ingles*). In recent years it has found its niche at Colour Bussing ceremonies largely through its championing by Mrs. Joyce Tinlin. When is a chorus not a chorus? When it is written by Tom Ker. In all three of his songs, published in the 2001 anthology, Ker purports to write a chorus, but it is only a chorus to the extent that he wishes everyone to join in at a certain juncture. For each verse of the song, his chorus words are different, apart from, perhaps, the opening and ending phrases. Key: C Maj. Range: C-E⌐.

29. Finnie, David (b. 1960)

David Finnie, author and composer of *Old Mill Town* **(73)** was born in Edinburgh on 25th July, 1960. Educated at Hawick High School until the age of sixteen, he entered the printing trade with the Hawick firm of Richardson & Son while continuing studies at Napier College, Edinburgh. He is a committed socialist and member of the Labour Party and served as an election agent in 1987. He served on Hawick Community Council and was, during the late '80s, a member of the Scottish Advisory Committee of the Independent Broadcasting Authority – the watchdog for Independent Television at that time. He has, in his own words, 'had a lifetime interest in, and love of, music' and has written many songs, some of which (e.g. *Old Man's Seat, The Secret Of My Longing* and *The Callant Becomes The Cornet*) have a local theme. Other songs like *In My Corner* (about his father) reveal a very personal aspect of his creativity. As with some other Hawick composers his not inconsiderable output tends to have been engulfed by a single song, in this case, the outstanding success of his *Old Mill Town*, but this does not detract in any way from the quality of his lesser known pieces. He is also a recording artist with something always on the stocks, who, with his band '3D', has been very successful in generating and sustaining interest in live performances of his music.

30. Gibb, David S. (1933-2007)

David Scobbie Gibb was born at 5 Oliver Park, Hawick on 6th December, 1933. On leaving Hawick High School at the age of fifteen, he entered Hawick's time-honoured industry as an apprentice in the underwear stockroom of Braemar Knitwear. This was interrupted by National Service in the Royal Air Force, but on his return to Braemar, after serving in various departments, he became one of the company's sales representatives for Scotland. Health problems, however, forced him to abandon travelling and in 1976 he joined the Hawick accountancy firm of John J. Welch & Co. where he served until his retirement. In a different age David Gibb might have gone to university. He was highly intelligent, astute and good with figures, but his main leisure interest was music. Possessed of an extraordinarily fine bass voice, he brought much pleasure to his fellow Borderers in Hawick and its environs, singing at concerts, soirees, residential care homes and voluntary associations and, of course, in his church activities over half a century, all of which was recognised in his being designated MBE in 2002. No surprise, then, that he was a member of Hawick Amateur Operatic Society, a founder member of Hawick Music Club in 1951 and a long-standing member of Hawick P.S.A. Male Voice Choir, in which he served as president (twice), secretary and treasurer. He performed with Carlisle's Abbey Singers and toured with them on the continent, in addition to which he was also a member of the Border Television Choir. Throughout his life, he was committed to the Church of Scotland, firstly at St. Andrew's, Hawick and, following its amalgamation with St. John's and East Bank in 1959, Trinity. He was a highly respected elder and treasurer of Trinity Church at the time of his death. Apart from this, he was committed to Hawick and in regular demand at Common Riding and Callants' Club functions and it was his honour to bang the bass drum in the Saxhorn Band as it led the Cornet and his followers in procession from the Volunteer Park in completion of the Mosspaul Ride. A regular favourite at Colour Bussing ceremonies, he excelled in his renditions of *Up Wi' The Banner* **(96)**, *Pawkie Paiterson* **(77)** and *Clinty* **(18)**, a role which he played with equal distinction in the 2000 revival of J.E.D. Murray's **(70)** melodrama *The Gutterbludes. Hawick Lasses 1514* **(40)** was David Gibb's only foray into composition. He died at Borders General Hospital on 14th January, 2007 and his ashes lie in Wilton Cemetery.

31. Goodfellow, George L. (b. 1951)

George Lamont Goodfellow was born in Hawick on 10th August, 1951 and was reared in the post-War prefabs of Silverbuthall. His early musical education (from the age of seven) took the form of piano lessons, which generated little enthusiasm, but after an adolescent dalliance with a set of drums, he settled down with an acoustic guitar and worked the scene as a member of contemporary folk groups 'Nemesis' and 'Bogard', which saw him develop a *penchant* for song writing in that style. His *Hawick Stands Alone* **(42)** is a good representative example of his craft. His work has found great acceptability in the USA where he became a member of the Tennessee Songwriters' Association. On leaving Hawick High School, George trained as a gas engineer and it is as such that he is known by most Teries. A proud supporter of all that makes Hawick Hawick, his membership of the Callants' Club, Hawick Archaeological Society and the very unique Anvil Crew[21] bespeaks his inborn affection for his native town.

32. Gotterson, Matthew (1828-1905)

Had J.E.D. Murray **(70)** been heeded, this name would be written 'Matthew Gotterson' (with special attention to the inverted commas) for it is, in fact, the pseudonym of James Smail who was born in Jedburgh on 1st November, 1828. He may have started his working life as a tailor. His career in banking began in 1852 at the National Bank in Jedburgh where his organisational abilities were recognised and he was selected in 1862 to open the Earlston branch of the Commercial Bank of Scotland, a task which he repeated at Galashiels in 1866. 1880 saw him as the bank's agent (manager) in Kirkcaldy and in 1884 he reached the exalted position of Secretary of the Commercial Bank of Scotland in Edinburgh, in which post he remained until his retirement in 1896. It is, however, as a ballad writer that Smail is best known. In these he managed to capture the essence and spirit of the old minstrels to the extent that many believed his verses were indeed those of the old minstrels themselves. His *Little Jock Elliot* is given as an example in *The Border Magazine* (May, 1896) under his own name, but when it was published as a piece of sheet music by his brother, Thomas

Smail, printer and bookseller of 16 High Street, Jedburgh, the words were attributed to none other than 'Matthew Gotterson'. After much fruitless research at the time of publication of the revised Hawick song anthology (2001), Ian Seeley **(86)**, its editor, and Ian Landles **(62)** concluded that Gotterson *had* to be J.E.D. Murray so the dates given for 'Matthew Gotterson' in that volume are erroneous.[22] They should have known better. Murray had far more confidence in his own work than anonymity would permit. Problem solved. Smail's poem, *The Hawick Callant* is surely not his best effort, which is probably why Adam Ingles **(55)** decided to set only one verse of it. It appeared in full in the first booklet of *Hawick Songs and Recitations* published by James Edgar in 1892, having appeared in *The Scotsman* and the *Hawick Advertiser* some three years earlier. Smail contributed verse and articles in prose to various magazines and newspapers, among them, *Chambers' Journal*, *The Border Magazine* and *The Scotsman.* Despite his rise to high office, Smail remained a Borderer through and through. He was an avid fisherman and his poems reflect his love of the Border hills, streams and historical sites. He was also a committed Volunteer, having joined the Kelso Company on its inception in 1859 – an interest he continued while resident in Earlston and Galashiels. James Smail died, aged 76, at 8 Bruntsfield Crescent, Morningside, Edinburgh on 22nd January, 1905 and was buried in that city's Grange Cemetery.

33. Grant, Adam (1859-1938)

Though reared in the Stockbridge district of Edinburgh, Adam Grant[23] was a native of St. Andrews – born in the town's Market Street on 1st April, 1859. At the age of twelve he was apprenticed to the Royal Warrant holding firm of Hamilton and Müller, Edinburgh, as an organ builder and piano tuner. It was a craft that required him to gain a measure of musical literacy and keyboard competency, but it was very much a case of 'learning on the job' and it is clear from his later compositions that he had not had the benefit of formal musical education. In other words, he was largely self-taught. Grant arrived in Hawick at the beginning of November, 1878, at the age of nineteen, to take up the post of organist at St. Cuthbert's Episcopal Church, where he remained until 1891 when he was appointed to St. John's in Oliver Crescent in the same capacity – a position he retained until 1936 – a remarkable forty five years' service to one congregation. In addition to his organist work, Grant advertised piano tuition and maintenance and, from May, 1882, established himself as a music seller, sharing a shop with another three merchants at 2 High Street (a handsome bronze plaque commemorating this enterprise was unveiled on the wall of this address by Cornet George Young in 1999). In 1885, he moved his business to 10 Bridge Street and lived with his wife and young family in the flat above the shop. And so Grant's Music Warehouse, which was to have so much influence on the musical scene in Hawick for the following fifty years, was born. Grant provided a comprehensive service: he sold pianos, organs and smaller instruments; he offered instrumental maintenance and tuning; he sold sheet music and gramophone records and also acted as a booking agent for performances at the Exchange, the Town Hall and the Croft Road Theatre (the 'Wee Thea'); but, most importantly, from the Hawick song point of view, he composed, published and compiled Hawick songs – the last of these activities being arguably the most important. Whether by accident or design arising from business acumen, Grant's decision to bind individual copies of Hawick songs into one volume ensured their material survival, lessening the danger of single sheets being thrown out for reasons of death, removal or general clearing out. The idea wasn't original; it was commonplace before the First World War to bind in one volume, for example, music hall songs or piano favourites; Grant simply applied a system that he knew worked, and he included in his local anthologies publications by Kennedys, Mozart Allan and Patersons as well as his own. To say that Adam Grant served Hawick's Common Riding related functions well would be to understate his commitment to Hawick. The first report we have of him as accompanist for the Colour Bussing is 1896 (Cornet Dr. Robert Mair); his final appearance as accompanist for this ceremony was in 1937 (Cornet Lockie Thorburn) – a span of forty one years' service. He was also accompanist to Hawick Callants' Club from its inception in 1903 until 1937. As a composer and arranger, Grant's contribution to Hawick song remains unmatched. All his songs and arrangements are sung – *Hawick* (**37**), *Up Wi' Auld Hawick* (**95**), *Oor Ain Auld Toon* (**75**), *Clinty's Song* (**18**), *Meda's Song* (**68**), *The Wail Of Flodden* (**97**) and *Invocation* (**57**). Taken together with his arrangements of *I Like Auld Hawick* (**53**), *I Like Auld Hawick The Best* (**54**), *Bonnie Teviotdale* (**11**), *The Anvil Crew* (**2**), *Kinly Stick* (**60**) and *Pawkie Paiterson* (**77**) this forms the foundation of the Hawick collection. Grant's friendship with J.E.D. Murray (**70**) saw him produce incidental music for the latter's plays – *The Caddie's Ghost*, *The Witch O' The Wisp Hill*, *Kirsty O' Cocklaw Castle*, *The Gutterbludes*, *Turning Back The Clock* and, of course the Hawick Quater-Centenary Historical Pageant (1914). *Meda's Song*, *Clinty's Song*, *The Wail Of Flodden* and *Invocation* apart, most of this music is now lost, but Hawick Saxhorn Band still plays the polka from *The Witch O' The Wisp Hill* in George Guy's[24] 1935 arrangement in *Memoirs Of Hawick*. Grant wrote one or two church anthems for St. John's but his only extant purely piano work is his *Branxholme Waltz* (written c. 1880 and dedicated to the Duchess of Buccleuch) which would seem to indicate that he was a pianist of considerable technical ability. Music apart, Grant was a keen Volunteer, a member (and sometime captain) of Teviotdale Amateur Bicycle Club, a member of Hawick Archaeological Society and of Hawick Golf Club.

He was also a Freemason, his lodge being St. John 111, his designation Grand Organist to the Provincial Grand Chapter of Roxburgh, Selkirk and Peebles. Throughout his time in Hawick he was always referred to as a man of great affability in his dealings with his fellow men in the 'grey auld toon'. Adam Grant died at Hillview, Southdean on 21st July, 1938 and was interred in Wellogate Cemetery.

34. Grant, Adam R. (1883-1952)

Adam Rutherford Grant was born at 18 High Street, Hawick on 4th March, 1883, the elder son of Adam Grant **(33)**, organist, composer, publisher and music dealer. Although he commenced work in the tweed industry, being of a musical disposition, he eventually followed his father into the family business at 10 Bridge Street. He was not a composer, however, and his musical memorial in Hawick is his renovation and resurrection of the two Ker/Grant songs *The Fairest Spot O' A'* **(28)** and *Where Slitrig And Teviot Meet* **(99)** in 1948 and 1949 respectively. In 1900 he became organist of Southdean Parish Church. He was organist at Bedrule when, in April, 1926 his father was invited to inaugurate that church's new pipe organ. In Edwardian times he ran a dance orchestra which played, among other venues, at the Masonic Fancy Dress Ball (10/11/1908) in St. John's Masonic Hall.[25] In 1920, Grant junior married into the Wallace family who farmed at Roundabouts, Bonchester Bridge, but although he went to live at Hillview, Southdean, he continued working with his father until the business was wound up in 1938. For the last fourteen years of his life, he continued to exert a musical presence in Hawick, accompanying at various Common Riding functions, etc. He became ill suddenly while on a visit to the Glasgow Hawick Association on 30th May, 1952 and was transferred to Stobhill Hospital where he died a week later on 6th June. His remains were cremated in Glasgow (Maryhill).

35. Halliday, John (1821-1902)

John Halliday was born by the Allan Water at a spot known as Hawickshiels, some four miles south of Hawick, on 18th June, 1821. He probably had no more than two years' schooling and, around the age of ten, he was hired by a local farmer as an assistant shepherd. He began writing verse when he was thirteen and at twenty was submitting poems to provincial periodicals. In 1849, he moved to Hobkirk where he was employed in draining, ditching, hedging and harvesting. In 1851 he was living and working at North Town o' Rule; in 1854 he was working at Bridge of Allan, near Stirling, as a landscape gardener and florist. Following the death of his wife in 1877, he moved to Stirling in 1893 to live with relatives at the Castle Hotel where he was reported to have enjoyed a 'vigorous and hearty old age, his interest in literature, especially poetry, being unabated.'[26] When he was resident at Longbaulk in 1847, he published a volume of poems and songs under the title *The Rustic Bard or A Voice From The People, Being Miscellaneous Poems and Songs.* These 351 pages of poetry plus a lengthy dedication and preface expounding his philosophy ('dedicated to the Working Classes of Scotland', etc.), which were published by James Brown, Galashiels, give some indication of his creativity. The poet's inspiration comes, in the main, from country life. He is today remembered in Hawick for his beautiful love song for all seasons, *Bonnie Teviotdale* **(11)**, which does not appear in that volume. Halliday died at Stirling on 16th January, 1902 and was buried at Logie, near Bridge of Allan, where a handsome memorial stone marks his grave.

36. Hartop, Kerr (b. 1996)

Surely the youngest published contributor to the Hawick song tradition for many decades (John Huggan **(49)** was, perhaps, the last, in 1932) Kerr Hartop was born in Melrose on 3rd January, 1996. From an established Hawick family (his great uncle, Tom Hartop, was the Cornet's Acting Father in 1981), it seems entirely appropriate that he should pen *The Best O' A'* **(9)** while still at school, creating something which his school music teacher, James Letham **(65)**, thought worthy of setting to music and which one primary school (Wilton) choir conductor thought worthy of performance at the 1514 Club's 'Hawick Sings' concert in 2012. See entry **9**.

37. Hawick

This vigorous song with words by James Logie Hercus **(44)**, an Orcadian, no less, and original music by Adam Grant **(33)**, made its debut at the Colour Bussing of 1898. The *Hawick News* (17/6/1898) recorded its 'pleasure' in a 'new song' entitled *Hawick*, 'the words by J.L. Hercus, and the music by M. Rosenberg **(82)** ...the song, which was finely rendered at the Colour Bussing by Mr. R. Paterson, is a very pleasing and tuneful composition, and well worthy of attention. The publisher is our townsman, Mr. A. Grant.' Grant and Rosenberg were, of course, one in the same person. Between 1898 and the Second World War the song appeared on no less than eighteen different Colour Bussing programmes. It is very much a 'singer's song' which has beguiled some of Hawick's most distinguished singers, among them John Campbell, who was for many years, president of Hawick Amateur Operatic Society (and a professionally trained bass) and Robert T. Roddan, the Borders Music Festival gold medallist of 1930. This song needs to be more than just 'sung'. It requires a performance. The words are powerful and replete with historical sentiment; the music is powerful; and its inclusive chorus soul stirring. In the right hands it can be devastating. The music is in the chordal style with which

Grant was most comfortable (compare with *Clinty's Song* **(18)**). Adam Ingles **(55)**, in 1957, removed, or simplified, some of Grant's running passages in the bass line of the piano part and took the song down by a tone from G Major, but, by and large, the song stands as the composer conceived it, losing none of its dynamism and vigour. *Hawick* forms the opening arrangement in George Guy's band medley, *Memoirs of Hawick* (1935). Key: F Maj. Range: C-D⌐.

38. Hawick Among The Hills

The upbeat mood of this song has made it a favourite at most Hawick Nights. The words, by John Inglis (1838-1928) **(56)**, form an exhortation to his *émigré* poet friend and fellow Teri, James Winthrope of Carleton Place, Toronto, to seek creative inspiration in his memories of Hawick ('*Look back on bonnie Teviotdale and Hawick among the hills*'). In 1887, another Hawick man, William Inglis Robson (1853-1891) **(81)** (then resident in Glasgow), composed music specifically for these words, so giving us the song we know today.[27] Prior to this, the song had been sung to Peter McLeod's (1797-1859) stirring tune to Henry Scott Riddell's *Scotland Yet!* The song, sung to that tune, had been around for many years before Miss. Nellie Anderson rendered the Robson version at the Council Chamber Colour Bussing ceremony of 1887 (see also note 27). Indeed, the *Hawick Express* (11/5/1878) carried a report of 'Mr. John Inglis...singing by desires, a song of his own composition – entitled 'Hawick Among the Hills'' at a farewell function for a Mr. Routledge in Wilton Old Church. Robson's melodic powers cannot be denied, but his original accompaniment has been altered considerably by Adam Ingles, largely, in the writer's opinion, for the better. The original is blighted by florid Victorian passage work along with 'symphonies' and interludes that are cluttered with tasteless arpeggiated triplets in the left hand. (Robson's work simply reflects a style that was commonplace among minor Victorian composers. It can also be observed, to some extent, in Taylor's **(91)** and even Francis George Scott's **(84)** original Hawick piano scorings). *Hawick Among The Hills* was originally published by W. & J. Kennedy, Hawick. Again, Ingles has taken this song down a tone from its original key of D Major. Key: C Maj. Range: B♭-E♭.

39. Hawick Callant, The

This song is mentioned in entry **32**. The words, by 'Matthew Gotterson', alias James Smail (1828-1905), were published in *The Hawick Advertiser* on 25th May, 1889 and recited at the Colour Bussing twelve days later (6th June 1889) by Mr. A. S. Lawson, junior. The full five verses were reprinted by James Edgar in his *Hawick Songs and Recitations* (1892). It was also published in the *Scotsman* in 1889. Adam Ingles **(55)** chose to set only verse 3 to music just after the Second World War – an insightful decision, because the quality of the other four is wanting compared with his choice. Ingles did, however, produce a robust melody consistent with the sentiment of his chosen words and that, in itself, is the mark of a discerning song composer. It is a short piece consisting of only sixteen bars without introduction. Indeed, it has become the custom to treat the song itself as an introduction to the first song at a Callants' Club function. The 'led in' song in recent years (announced by the president as 'a song of his (the singer's) choice') has, in recent years, invariably been *The Border Queen* **(12)**, but there is no good reason, given the exhortation from the Chair, why that choice shouldn't change from time to time. *The Hawick Callant* is, in effect, the Callants' Club club song which opens the entertainment at their social functions. Key: G Maj. Range: D-E♭.

40. Hawick Lasses 1514

The poem of this title first appeared in the *Hawick Express* of 8th June, 1928 and is the work of James Y. Hunter (1877-1937) **(50)**, a Hawick man who was, at that time, headmaster of Cellardyke Primary School, near Anstruther in Fife. In the decade prior to his death, he made a point of sending a Common Riding or 1514 commemorative poem to the local press around Common Riding time. David Gibb **(30)** conceived the melody for this song and submitted it to the Callants' Club committee tasked with bringing the 2001 edition of the *The Hawick Songs – A Complete Collection* to fruition, but it has to be admitted that its possible inclusion in this volume presented problems (all contributions and suggestions were subjected to rigorous scrutiny). Though not without merit, the melody tends to wander and, in some ways, seems to struggle for direction, but doubtless, in the hands of a performer of David Gibb's calibre, the song could work well. Given the number of Hawick songs available to singers who, realistically, seek some kind of personal *cachet* from a performance, this song may, however, struggle for a champion. It has, to our knowledge, never had a public performance. The piano accompaniment was devised by Ian Seeley, as editor of the anthology. The song was recorded by Gibb shortly before his death and is included on Hawick Callants' Club's CD – *Hawick and Teviotdale in Song and Poetry.* Key: G/D Maj. Range: D-D|.

41. Hawick Reivers

This song was written at the end of August, 1995; words and music were conceived simultaneously. *Hawick Reivers* is the fourth of Ian Seeley's **(86)** five Hawick songs written between 1994 and 1996. It was dedicated to Seeley's friend, Salvationist J. Elliot Renwick, who printed and published the first four songs at the Buccleuch Printers, Carnarvon Street – of which he was co-director. This is a vigorous song which suggests the urgency of a raid. The use of the minor key brings to it a certain commanding starkness which reflects the warlike spirit of the words. Seeley makes no concession to popularity in his songs. They have no chorus and are basically art songs, written by a professional musician and not aimed at the novice performer. The Hawick tenor, Elliot Goldie, recorded *Hawick Reivers* and it proved sufficiently successful for the song book committee to confirm its inclusion in the 2001 anthology, but, as with most of Seeley's songs, it is a moot point as to how often it will be performed. Attractive and clever it may be in the hands of an accomplished performer, but there are many far more accessible Hawick songs. Key: D Min. Range: A_1-D^1.

42. Hawick Stands Alone

This song, taken within the Hawick song context, could be described as a 'one-off' or a mould-breaker in the same way that Neil McKay's **(68)** *Home By Burnfoot* **(47)** forced the Common Riding musical fraternity to draw in a deep breath. Hawick songs just weren't written like that and followed the more traditional approach either as an updated drawing room ballad or as a pseudo-Scottish folk song like, for example, Julius Mickles's *There's Nae Luck Aboot The Hoose*. The very thought of a Hawick song with overtones of country and western music! But *Hawick Stands Alone* is an excellent example of George Goodfellow's **(31)** preferred musical style, used, in this case, as a vehicle for retelling the 1514 story; and it works remarkably well, if only singers will give it a chance. Originally conceived with guitar accompaniment, it was felt that, for the wider purposes of the 2001 anthology, a piano accompaniment would be required. The editor of that volume devised the accompaniment as given. Key: G Maj. Range: D-D^1.

43. Hawick Volunteers

On 12th May, 1859, the British Secretary of State for War, Jonathan Peel, issued a circular letter to the lieutenants of the English, Welsh and Scottish counties, authorising the formation of volunteer rifle corps to act as a kind of citizens' army for the protection of the nation in the event of a French invasion. Officers were to be appointed by the lord lieutenants and the detachments were to be fairly autonomous yet affiliated to the regular army. It is not surprising that the lord lieutenants looked for leaders who were already established as leaders in their communities either by rank, civic achievement or as industrial magnates (the self-made men, or *nouveaux riches*). In 1860 (the year of the formation of the Hawick corps) Bailie George Hardy Fraser was one of them and he was the brother-in-law of Lindsay Watson of the highly successful Hawick firm of William Watson & Sons, tweed makers. So it was that the recently formed Hawick Rifle Volunteers were granted the use of Watsons' newly constructed mill flat for a concert on 13th December, 1860. At that concert, George Fraser sang *Our Hawick Volunteers*, newly penned with due topicality by Hawick's adopted son, James Thomson **(94)**. The melody, presumably selected by Thomson, was that of *The Red Cross Banner*, which Adam Ingles **(55)** claims 'was *undoubtedly* a hymn tune, popular about that time.' It is, in fact, a 'national' song dating from 1841, composed by Sidney Nelson (1800-1862) to words by W. H. Bellamy and published by Cramer, Addison & Beale, London. Nelson was a popular English Victorian drawing room ballad composer whose claim to fame today is the two 'Scots' songs he wrote with his fellow countryman Charles Jefferys (1807-1865) – *Mary of Argyle* and *The Rose of Allandale.* He was an authority on vocal production, and that same *penchant* for the use of melodic ornamentation (particularly the turn), which is so much a feature of *Mary of Argyle,* is evidenced in *The Red Cross Banner* (the melody appropriated by Thomson for *Hawick Volunteers*). *Hawick*

Volunteers evokes a 'Classical' style with its use of melodic ornamentation (the turn) and its overall symmetry, i.e. balancing phrases. The song has a certain grand elegance reminiscent of the 'national' patriotic songs of Thomas Arne and John Wall Callcott (cf. *Rule, Britannia!* and *Ye Mariners of England* respectively). Although, chronologically, it is the fourth song created specifically for Hawick, it has struggled to capture public attention, possibly because it carries no reference to Hawick's illustrious past. Even the Volunteers did not espouse *Our Hawick Volunteers* as their company marching song, preferring instead, General Reid's[28] *In The Garb Of Old Gaul. Hawick Volunteers*, as the song is now known, appears from time to time on Hawick concert programmes as a curiosity, although, interestingly, at the height of the Boer War, it made the Colour Bussing of 1900 when it was sung by Thomas Scott. Key: C Maj. Range: C#-E♭.

44. Hercus, James L. (1847-1885)

James Logie Hercus was born in Albert Street, Kirkwall, Orkney, in 1847[29] and educated at Kirkwall Grammar School, following which he may have worked for a short time with his father, a house painter. In 1868 he was resident at 12 Colville Place, Stockbridge, Edinburgh, in which city he met his future wife, a Borders girl – Joan Jamieson Laidlaw – so also beginning a love affair with the Borders. They married at Morebattle on 31st December, 1868. The 1871 Census records them at 54 Albert Street, Glasgow and his occupation as law clerk. He died, aged 38, at 1 Firpark Terrace, Dennistoun, Glasgow on Christmas Day, 1885 and was buried at Morebattle, on the Scottish Border. He wrote numerous poems (there are sixty six in the volume of his collected poems – *Songs of the Borderland and Other Verses*) about the Borders, but his *Minto Crags, Dr. John Leyden* and *Hawick On The Border*[30] are the only ones which relate to the Hawick district. It is the last of these (with shortened title *Hawick*) which has become his memorial in Hawick in its fine 1898 musical setting by Adam Grant **(33)**, alias M. Rosenberg **(82)**.

45. Hogg, Frank (1840-1880)

Francis (Frank) Hogg was born at Drinkstone Cottage in the Parish of Wilton in 1840, the son of an agricultural labourer of the same name. He became a solicitor's clerk with the firm of George & James Oliver in Hawick, and lived at 1 Allars Bank. He was an enthusiastic and popular member of Hawick Archaeological Society, becoming its treasurer over a period of twelve years. Ever interested in pursuits of the mind, he worked tirelessly for the precursor of what we know today as the Public Library which, at that time, operated from the Exchange. He was a member of Hawick Literary Society, writing for its magazine in 1867 the poem which would ensure his memory in the 'grey auld toon' – *I Like Auld Hawick* **(53)**. He became ill suddenly at the Exchange Hall and died there on 7th February, 1880, aged 40. He was buried in Wilton Cemetery. One measurement of the affection with which he was held in Hawick is that, in the year following his death, a street – Frank Place[31] – was named after him. He is the only Hawick song writer to have achieved this distinction, *post mortem* or otherwise!

46. Hogg, James (1780-1838)

Our man should not be confused with the poet and novelist of the same name, sometimes known as 'The Ettrick Shepherd' (1770-1835) and, clearly contemporaneous with him. Hawick's James Hogg was born in the town around 1780 and began his working life as a shepherd on the upper reaches of the Teviot. He was later apprenticed as a stocking maker and, being of technical bent, distinguished himself in the trade by devising improvements to the knitting frame and its use. He invented the welt to rib stocking tops. He was a campaigner for the rights of the working man in what was then a fairly young industry and suffered imprisonment in Jedburgh Jail in 1832 for his pains. Trade unionism, even in its most elementary form, was considered a crime. Hogg was a member of the West End Congregation, under Dr. Young and Mr. Rodgie. Like many working class men of his period (the post-Classical and early Romantic periods in Scotland) he was consumed by the desire for learning and self-improvement, and spent much of what leisure time he had poring over books dealing with science, technology, and, of course, our national cultural heritage of poetry, legend and song. Balbirnie's *Old Song* **(74)** impressed him deeply; of that there can be no doubt, because his 'new' song – *The Colour* **(20)** – our current *Teribus* **(92)**, 'shadows' the style of the old. The *guarding/defending* of the Common and the rights associated with it are common to both songs, as are some of the epithets (e.g. *'martial order'* and the idea of Hawick *forever/was ever independent'* in the last verses). But the main differences are contextual. Balbirnie's song is more socio-geographical. He reminds us why we are doing this commemoration, but he also takes us on a tour of the Common Riding of his day. Hogg, on the other hand, takes a historico-legendary approach and his verse is less clumsy. Hogg's poem was published in 1819 as one part of a larger entity which included *Flodden Field* and both were sung at the Common Riding that year by one James Scott[32] (a former apprentice of Hogg) to the tune *Teribus*. Robert Murray opines that they were 'the loving labour of many years.' Hogg's place in the annals of Hawick song was secured. His other three extant poems are *An Address To The Inhabitants Of Hawick* (1809), *Carterhaugh Ba`* (1815) and *Lament On The Death Of Rob Reid Of Roadhead`s Dog Flora.* He died suddenly at 14 Loan, Hawick on 3rd November, 1838 in his 58th year. A plaque (incidentally, with the *wrong* date of death[33]) on the wall of the present-day building at that address commemorates his life. He was buried in Old Wilton Cemetery.

47. Home By Burnfoot

At its meeting on 8th January, 1970, Burnfoot Residents' Association resolved to instigate a competition for a new song, which 'would be open to anyone and must have Burnfoot and the Common Riding as its theme.' A double column advertisement in the *Hawick Express* (14/1/1970) detailed 'The entries, which should contain a Common Riding theme with emphasis on Burnfoot, will compete for a trophy suitably inscribed, and will be judged by audience reaction at a special concert along the lines of the *Opportunity Knocks*[34] show, at Burnfoot. Entries should be in (or notified) to the song Committee Chairman, Mr. J. Kinghorn...' In due course, the same newspaper announced on its front page (24/5/1970) that three songs had been listed, two of them by already known Common Riding/Hawick song writers (Adam Ingles **(55)**/David Johnston **(58)** and Mrs. Jenny (Janet) Smith **(88)**, a teacher at Drumlanrig St. Cuthbert's Primary School) and one by Neil Mackay **(66)**, at that time Hawick Town Councillor for the ward of Burnfoot. The winning song was to be sung in Burnfoot Roadhouse on the return of the Cornet from Denholm. In the event, the trophy went to Councillor Mackay for his *Home By Burnfoot*, sung by 'six young ladies from Burnfoot.' The song won because it was a breath of fresh air – something as different from the traditional concept of a 'Hawick song' as could be imagined. It was catchy, some would say 'cheeky', pure *vaudeville*, in fact, and entirely in line with what the Burnfoot Song Committee had stipulated. However, these very attributes also brought it the status of a 'one off', a direction changer and even a threat to the status quo, and while it may have been successful at Burnfoot, the Common Riding fraternity treated it with an indifference akin to the Thatcherian concept of 'not one of us.' Apart from performances relating to Burnfoot, its appearances on programmes at Common Riding functions in general are sparse. Robert Hume, erstwhile Bandmaster of Hawick Saxhorn Band, has given the melody a boost in one of his band medleys (it makes a very fine march) and Ian Seeley has performed it in arrangement as a piano burlesque, but like several other Hawick songs (which are not half as original) it is in need of a champion. Musically, Mackay's melody is simple in conception, consisting of an eight bar, non-modulating melody which is then simply repeated as a chorus (very similar, in fact, to the form of *The Anvil Crew* **(2)**). Key: F Maj. Range: C-D♩.

48. Hornshole

This pleasant piece comes from the versatile pen of Ian Landles **(62)**. It was written for the Official Song-singer, Michael Aitken, as part of an entertainment given by the author/composer at Thorterdykes Roadhouse on 10th September, 2008. The sentiments expressed have been well aired as a reminder of why Hawick does this commemoration every June. The music actually constitutes a slow foxtrot and is of ternary construction, that is, threefold – a main melody followed by a contrasting melody and eventual return to the main melody (AABA). The piano accompaniment was devised by Ian Seeley. Key: F Maj. Range: C-E♩.

49. Huggan, John (1914-1989)

John Huggan was born at 28 Wellogate Place, Hawick, on 19th August, 1914, but was reared at 8 Gladstone Street, and later, in Mansfield Road. On leaving Hawick High School he was employed by Innes, Henderson & Co., but factory life was never going to suit him and he had an escape route – music, at which he excelled. A pupil of Adam Colledge **(19)** and later, David B. Simpson FRCO, the distinguished organist of St. George's (now Teviot) Church, he went on to take the LRAM and LTCL diplomas which enabled him in 1936 to quit the knitwear industry for teacher training at Moray House Training College in Edinburgh. He remained organist of St. John's Church (where he had followed Adam Grant) during this period but, after qualifying in

1937, departed Hawick for a teaching post in Buckie, Banffshire, where he remained until, in 1940, he registered for war service in the Royal Air Force. After demobilisation in 1946, he was appointed Principal Teacher of Music in Galashiels Academy, a post he retained until his retirement in 1974 and during the tenure of which he gained the ARCO diploma in 1951. He taught piano in Roxburghshire schools for a further two years, but in 1976 took up residence at 4 Gillsland Road, Edinburgh. John Huggan was a modest man who tended to underplay his undoubted musical ability. It is therefore not surprising that he was reticent about giving Adam Ingles **(55)** permission to include what he considered to be his youthful, immature song – *The Exile's Dream* **(26)** in the 1957 song anthology. John Huggan died, aged 75, at Edinburgh Royal Infirmary on 18th December, 1989 and was cremated at Mortonhall, Edinburgh.

50. Hunter, James Y. (1877-1937)

James Young Hunter was born at 4 Brougham Place, Hawick on 4th April, 1877, the eldest son of Robert Hunter **(51)**, factory manager and poet (cf. *Oor Bonnie Border Toon* **(76)**). He was educated at Buccleuch School (now Hawick High School) and then at the Free Church Training College, Edinburgh after which, in 1899, he was appointed an assistant teacher in Drumlanrig Public School. He graduated MA at Edinburgh University in April, 1900, subsequently holding teaching posts in Dalbeattie and St. Andrews before being appointed headmaster, first at Lundin Links and, finally, at Cellardyke. He really was the epitome of the 'lad o' pairts' – the all-rounder. In 1905, he took first prize in the Agriculture and Rural Economy Class at St. Andrews University. He was an extremely popular teacher of continuation classes while at St. Andrews where, on 12th April, 1909 he was the recipient of a presentation from his students, who lauded him for his 'untiring energy and tactful treatment of the students'. In the last decade of his life, he was the annual contributor of a Common Riding poem, at that time of year, to the *Hawick Express. Hawick Lasses 1514* **(40)** appeared in June 1928, but other years elicited from his pen such poems as *June Fever, The Ca' Knowe, Sing Me A Song, A Hawick Song* and *Heart's Hame O' The Callant*, which William Landles **(63)**, writing in the Edinburgh *Evening News*, early in 1937, reckoned was his masterpiece. He wrote it for, and recited it at, the Colour Bussing of 1899. James Hunter was found dead in bed on the morning of 18th August, 1937 while on holiday at the Waverley Hotel, Crieff. He was 60 years of age. His grave is in the Western Cemetery, St. Andrews.

51. Hunter, Robert (1854-1905)

The author of *Oor Bonnie Border Toon* **(76)**, Robert Hunter,[35] was born in Hawick on 21st January, 1854. On leaving school, he went into the tweed industry with Messrs. William Watson & Sons, Dangerfield Mills, training as a power loom tuner. He worked away from Hawick for a spell in Banff and Carlisle and, on his return to the town, took up a position with Messrs .Wilson and Glenny where he was mill manager for twenty five years. He was the epitome of Victorian rectitude – an elder of East Bank Church, Sunday School teacher, president of the Band of Hope and of Hawick Total Abstinence Society. He was also a member of Hawick Archaeological Society. The measure of his abilities in poetry was recognised when, in 1879, he entered a poetry competition on the statue of Burns in Dumfries and, from thirty two competitors, was awarded second place. His literary reputation in Hawick today is centred on three poems – *Oor Bonnie Border Toon, The Auld Man's Common Riding* and *Hark Again The Stirring Strain* (*Hawick Common Riding*) with its memorable last verse – *It`s no' in steeds, it's no' in speeds, It's something in the heart abiding...*' A Freemason, he was Bard of Lodge St. John 111. Robert Hunter died, four days short of his fifty first birthday, on 17th January, 1905 at 13 Beaconsfield Terrace, Hawick and was buried in Wellogate Cemetery.

52. Hurrah! For The Cornet

This song was a piece of education in practice in which a teacher, Mrs. Janet Smith **(88)**, did what all good teachers try to do – create enthusiasm by making their subject topical and relevant to the immediate environment of their pupils. The immediate environment in May for many primary school pupils in Hawick is the rising enthusiasm for the approaching Common Riding and the Cornet's visits to the schools, where he is cheered to the echo as he requests the head teacher to grant the holiday from the time of his departure. It's all part of the ritual, of course, because the education authority has already agreed with schools across the region which local public holidays will be taken, but for the children, it ramps up 'June fever' – and this was the song for the Cornet's visit to Drumlanrig Primary School in 1968. The pupils, under Mrs. Smith's guidance, contributed to a formulation of words for which she then provided a melody. Drumlanrig School Log Book entry for 6th June, 1968 details – ' P5 pupils wrote the words of a new song *Hurrah for the Cornet* and Mrs. Smith the music. This was sung in public for the first time today and greeted with warm applause and appreciation by all who heard it.' It is a school song for young people to sing and that is what it will remain. It was described on the front page of the *Hawick Express* (5/6/1968) as 'a song specifically for children by children.' Well, almost. It has been sung in recent years at the 1514 Club's 'Hawick Sings' concerts, fittingly, by choirs from Drumlanrig Primary School, to an accompaniment devised by Ian Seeley in 2006. Key: C/F Maj. Range: C-E♭.

53. I Like Auld Hawick

These are the only words by Frank Hogg **(45)** to be transformed into a song, and this happy union of words and music resulted from the inspiration kindled in Mrs. Euphemia Dumbreck **(24)** of Teviotside House private school.[36] The melody which she provided remains one of the most loved in the Hawick repertoire – a truly remarkable example, paradoxically, of the power of simplicity. A binary, or two-fold, melody with a straightforward textbook modulation half way through and an understated, but strong sequence in the second half gives the song melodic cohesion and direction. This is a song which can be sung convincingly by a male or female voice. We can be definite about the date of the words. Hogg wrote them in 1867 for Hawick Literary Society's MS Magazine. The date for the music (and hence, the song) is in all likelihood, between Summer, 1875 and three years later (1878). We know this because, on 12th June, 1875, the *Hawick Express* reprinted the full seven verses of the poem with a footnote declaring, 'we gladly give them publicity in our columns, and we should be happy to see if some of our local composers could popularise them by setting them to a suitable air.' Was it to this exhortation that Mrs. Dumbreck responded? If so, it is highly likely that the song was created within the following year (1876). A little more than two years later she was suffering from dementia and had to be cared for in the District Asylum at Melrose, where she died on 23rd November, 1879. *I Like Auld Hawick*, as a song, was definitely established some time before this because the author sang it himself at a farewell supper for Bailie Michie on the eve of his departure for South Africa, 26th September, 1879. Within the following five months, Hogg too had departed. Today, only verses 1, 2, and 7 (i.e. of Hogg`s original) are sung regularly, and, on very rare occasions, verse 4 (*'But they know not the spirit...'*). The fact is that, verses 1, 2 and 7 apart, the words of the remaining four are awkwardly matched to the melody. One

54

has to wonder, indeed, if three of them were ever sung. The song as it stands today is Adam Grant's **(33)** Edwardian arrangement (verses renumbered), which he re-issued *c.* 1930, and dedicated to Ex-Provost James Renwick. Key: G Maj. Range: B♭-E♭.

54. I Like Auld Hawick The Best

This song, with words and melody by Tom Ker **(59)**, was first described in the *Hawick Advertiser* (2/2/1900) as 'a song just published by Mr. Grant, musicseller. The words are by Mr. T. Ker and the music by Mr. M. Rosenberg. The piece should be secured by all musically inclined. It deserves wide publicity.' Perusal of Grant's publication shows very clearly that this song is 'Written & Composed by Tom Ker' and '*Arranged* by M. Rosenberg', who was, of course, none other than Grant himself. Indeed, Grant was later to reveal that, of all his Hawick *arrangements*, he considered this his best. It is noteworthy that he made no further Ker arrangements and showed no inclination to do so. This has always been a popular Hawick song. It was sung at the Colour Bussing of 1900 by Robert Telfer Paterson[37] and at no less than twenty three subsequent similar ceremonies by different singers (men and women) before the Second World War. It continues to rank as a favourite to this day. It is truly a song of praise – nothing, but nothing, no place, can beat Hawick for the beauty among which the town is situated and truly, Ker's melody is a glorious reflection of that, with an emotionally charged 'chorus' to boot. Ker's idea of a chorus is somewhat idiosyncratic and is detailed in entry **28**. Nevertheless, those who had the privilege of hearing this song performed by the late Mr. Viv Sharp know that such peculiarities will never be an impediment to an excellent song in the hands of a true performer. *I Like Auld Hawick The Best* is a song that has brought the house down on countless occasions and, doubtless, will continue to do so. Key: F Maj. Range: C-C♭.

55. Ingles, Adam L. (1914-1991)

Adam Little Ingles was, in physical stature, a small man, but a giant in terms of what he achieved for Hawick and the ethos and culture of its Common Riding. Like Adam Grant **(33)** before him, he was the most genial and generous of men – a disposition which enabled him to respect, and be respected by, people of widely differing opinions, so enabling him to sidestep conflict and get things done. This was most evident in the machinations leading up to the publication of *The Hawick Songs – A Complete Collection*, in 1957, when he had to deal with a potentially hostile Common Riding Committee and suspicious Hawick Callants' Club.[38] Adam Ingles was born (appropriately) on Common Riding morning, 5th June, 1914 at 7 Green Terrace, Hawick. He had piano tuition from a lady (Anne McCallum) who lived in the same street (in the old 'Green Kirk' Manse) and, aged thirteen, had organ lessons from George Smith ARCO, the organist of St. Cuthbert's Episcopal Church. Like many young musical Teries of that time, he would purchase his music in the characteristic aroma of pipe smoke that pervaded Adam Grant's **(33)** music shop at 10 Bridge Street. On leaving Hawick High School, where he was contemporary with John Huggan **(49)**, he started work as a joiner with the respected Hawick firm of Messrs. A. Inglis & Son, but this was short lived and he secured a position in the stock room of Innes, Henderson & Co. where he lasted four years before going into his father's business as a jeweller and watchmaker. (The latter served him well when, in 1941, he was called to military service in the Royal Air Force and assigned to flying instrument technology). On demobilisation, he undertook studies in Edinburgh and Glasgow to qualify as an optician, an occupation which he relished because, he said, he 'liked to help people.' His passions, however, were music and Hawick Common Riding. He became organist of St. Margaret's Church, (the site is now occupied by Langlands Court) at the age of 17 and served for four years before it was linked with Wilton South. A further twenty four years ensued at Wilton South before his departure for St. George's West in 1959. 1961 saw him at Hawick Old Parish Church (its site is now occupied by Frank Scott Court) for the next eight years, followed by a brief period at Hawick Trinity prior to Ian Seeley's **(86)** arrival there in 1970. In the very last years of his life, he was organist of St. Mary's, Hawick's spiritual shrine. Adam Ingles distributed his musical talent over so many institutions in Hawick that space here restricts specific listing, but it covered rugby clubs, forces' associations and the whole panoply of Common Riding affiliated clubs and associations – Hawick Callants' Club (of which he was president in 1976), The Ancient Order of Mosstroopers (president in 1967) and the 1514 Club, for which he initiated the 'Hawick Sings' concerts and composed the music for the club song – *We'll Follow Oor Cornet Roon'* **(98)**. He was a fully active participant in Hawick Common Riding, filling with distinction the role of Acting Father to Cornet Brydon in 1964. Adam Ingles, writing of Adam Grant **(33)** in his *Notes And Comments On The Songs Of Hawick* stated, 'We must thank Adam Grant more than anyone else for our wonderful heritage of Hawick songs'.[39] It is an accolade which, with minor modification to 'for preserving and building on Adam Grant's legacy', could be applied to Adam Ingles. Adam Grant will always be the bright shining star of Hawick song, but a star which required polishing at a certain point when its lustre seemed, after the Second World War, to have faded. Fortunately, Adam Ingles was on hand to do the job. His edition of the Hawick song collection in 1957 was a landmark and the matrix which spawned a whole new generation of Hawick songwriters led by Ingles himself. He should not, however, be above criticism. In spite of his assurances in 1955 to the Common Riding Committee that the songs would not be drastically altered save for a change of key here, or a tricky piano passage there, he pushed the boat out about as far as, at that time, it could go. Some of the songs (e.g. *The Mosstrooper's Song*) were still in copyright (it will be until 2035) but Ingles was not deterred in altering its accompaniment, let it be said, for the better. Perhaps he felt that Adam Colledge was easier to charm than the tetchy Francis George Scott, who made it clear that he would countenance no alterations whatsoever to *Oor Bonnie Border Toon.* The accompaniment of *The Banner Blue* (also still in copyright in 1957) was emasculated, becoming no more than a pale shadow of Taylor's intention. The accompaniment of Grant's *Meda's Song* was embellished because, as Ingles reveals in his *Notes And Comments*, from the accompanist's viewpoint, in his opinion, 'efforts at improvising to make the music fit the words, make the song more enjoyable.'[40] What cannot be disputed, however, is the fact that Ingles gave the Hawick songs a shot in the arm at the right moment. History is ever subject to revision. Adam Ingles, who also held the ATCL diploma, added some classics of his own to the Hawick repertoire, including *Auld Hawick, My Dreams* **(4)**, *Auld Hawick, Where I Was Born* **(5)**, *The Hawick Callant* **(39)**, *We'll Follow Oor Cornet Roon'* **(98)** and *Borthwick Water* **(13)**. A debt is owed to Adam Ingles for his pioneer work in tracing the history of the Hawick songs and their writers, much of which has inspired the present researches. Adam Ingles died at Hawick Cottage Hospital on the 27th July, 1991 and was buried in Wellogate Cemetery.

56. Inglis, John (1838-1928)

John Inglis was born in Drumlanrig Square,[41] Hawick on 23rd May, 1838 – a descendent of the Gledstanes of Cocklaw Castle and Hilliesland on his father's side and of the last ferryman of the Coble Pool on his mother's side – something which, throughout his long life, gave him enormous satisfaction and pride. His working life was spent in the tweed trade, firstly at Messrs. Wilson & Armstrong and then at Messrs. Wilson & Glenny where he was weft foreman. A committed churchman and elder of Wilton

Church, he was a lifelong abstainer. He was a member of the Border Bards Association, founded in Murray's Temperance Hotel at 15 High Street in 1878 which included, among its membership, Robert Hunter **(51)**. Poetry and church apart, his other interests were his membership of the Volunteers and of Hawick Archaeological Society. On his retiral from factory work he became curator of Hawick Museum when it was housed at the Buccleuch Memorial (opposite the present public library in Bridge Street) and, for the final twenty years of his life, at Wilton Lodge. His memory lives on in Hawick largely, if not exclusively, through the two song settings of his words, *Hawick Among The Hills* **(38)** (set by William Inglis Robson **(81)**) and *The Banner Blue* **(8)** (set by Joshua Taylor **(91)**). John Inglis died suddenly in his ninety-first year, at Wilton Lodge on 26th December, 1928 and was laid to rest in Wellogate Cemetery.

57. Invocation

This twelve-bar choral piece has all the characteristics of a German chorale – slow, stepwise melody and pauses, or implied pauses, at the end of each phrase. Adam Ingles **(55)**, in his *Notes and Comments on the Songs of Hawick*, draws our attention to its similarity (in the first phrase, at least) to *Nun danket alle Gott. Invocation*, or *The* Invocation, as Hawick people will insist, is indeed a parody of a German Lutheran hymn, even down to what Ingles called 'very extreme and unusual harmonies'. These harmonies are 'tame' when compared with some of J. S. Bach's chorale harmonisations of two centuries earlier. *Invocation* was created by J.E.D. Murray **(70)** and Adam Grant **(33)** to provide a fitting grand finale to the Hawick Quater-Centenary Historical Pageant, performed in the Volunteer Park on the evenings of 2nd and 3rd June,1914, when it was sung by vast numbers to the accompaniment of Hawick Saxhorn Band. A year later (1915) Grant published it. The *Hawick Express* (11/6/1915) informs us, '...at the moderate price of two-pence, it should have a large sale.' Its choral outings have been few since then, but it was rendered by Trinity Church Choir for the centenary commemoration service for the Callants' Club in 2004 and it was sung at the same venue for the Kirking of Cornet Nichol in 2012. Its principal ceremonial function has become its role on Common Riding Saturday afternoon when it is played by the Saxhorn Band outside the Town Hall as the Cornet hands back his flag to the Provost, 'unsullied and unstained' and his mounted supporters stand to attention in the High Street. Key: F Maj. Range: F-D$^{|}$.

58. Johnston, David (1900-1982)

The author of *We'll Follow Oor Cornet Roon'* **(98)** and *My Borderland* **(71)**, David Johnston, was born at 95 Roxburgh Street, Kelso on 2nd October, 1900 and educated at Kelso Public School. On leaving school he started work as a gardener at Floors Castle, but came to live in Hawick after meeting and marrying a Hawick girl. He lived latterly in its Burnfoot ward, where he became known as 'The Burnfit Bard.' He worked as a general handyman at Lyle & Scott's Burnfoot plant and also as a boilerman at the town's Victoria Laundry, which in no way dampened his pen. He was a regular contributor of verse to the local newspapers. He collaborated with composer Adam Ingles **(55)** on several occasions, but apart from these two songs (the latter by Albert Budge **(15)**), the results were disappointing. Their entry for the 'Song for Burnfoot' competition in 1970 faded into obscurity and an extant manuscript copy of a song entitled *Braw Border Queens* shows Ingles in need of more inspiring lyrics. A volume of his verses entitled *A Freen Among Freens* was published locally in 1974, achieving reasonable circulation, but his lasting poetical memorials will, in all probability, be *We'll Follow Oor Cornet Roon'* and *My Borderland* **(71)**. Predeceased by his wife, he moved to Arbroath to be near his son. David Johnston died at 54 Brechin Road, Arbroath on 7th August, 1982. His remains were interred in Wilton Cemetery, Hawick.

59. Ker, Tom (1856-1932)

Tom Ker was born at 32 The Square, Kelso on 4th July, 1856, but was reared in the schoolhouse of the Ragged, or Industrial, School (Drumlanrig), Hawick where his father was headteacher. On leaving school he trained as a draper with James Turnbull of 11 High Street, but soon entered the knitwear trade, firstly with John Laing & Sons, Slitrig Crescent, and then, for the rest of his career, with Robert Pringle & Sons, Ltd., for whom he became a travelling representative, covering Scotland, Ireland and the English Midlands. In his youth he was an ardent sportsman, engaging in cycling, cricket and rugby (he played in the first match in Hawick – Hawick v. Langholm – on 7/2/1874) and was captain of the Hawick squad 1877-78 and 1880-81 besides acting as their Secretary for three years. Musically inclined, he was a member of Hawick Choral Union, at that time under the conductorship of Charles Taylor (late 1870s). He relished singing at social gatherings, for example, at the meetings of the Teviotdale Amateur Bicycle Club, where, it would later be recalled, his own songs were sung, namely *The Fairest Spot O' A'* **(28)**, *Where Slitrig And Teviot Meet* **(99)** and, of course, *I Like Auld Hawick The Best* **(54)**. There is an alternative set of words to the last title, but it is seldom used. His interest in literary pursuits grew through the late-Victorian and Edwardian periods, and found him a regular contributor of verse to newspapers and magazines such as *The Border Magazine*, submitting his work under the pseudonym 'Tee Kay'. It was said that 'Tee Kay loved Hawick and Hawick loved Tee Kay.' The inscription on his headstone bears this out, being erected 'in grateful recognition of his personal worth, poetic gifts and public service to the community over half a century.' In 1900, he was elected a town councillor for the North High Street ward, in which capacity he served for twelve years until pressure of work forced his resignation. He was a founding member of Hawick Callants' Club in 1903, and became its first president. It was he who started the custom of honouring the chief guest at their annual dinner with an appropriately penned acrostic on the back of the menu. His pen was seldom idle. He wrote Episode 7 of the Hawick Quater-Centenary Historical Pageant – 'Hab o' Hawick' – in 1914 and, in 1924, was persuaded to issue a volume of his works – which he entitled *Some Thouchts O' Mine in Song and Verse.* This volume of sixty six poems and twenty six acrostics includes the songs already mentioned, and poems like *Gather, Callants, Gather* and the more serious *A Refuge From The Storm.* Ker was Secretary and Treasurer of Hawick Common Riding Committee over many years, and also a prominent Freemason whose connection was with Lodge St. John 111, of which he was Bard. In later life he lived for several years in Edinburgh, but as his health failed, he sought refuge in the home of his married daughter in Glasgow. It was there, at 28 Arlington Street, that he died, aged 76, on 19th November, 1932. His remains were brought back to Hawick by train and interred in Wellogate Cemetery.

60. Kinly Stick

This is William Easton's **(25)** other humorous Hawick song, concerning two Hawick reprobates in need of alcoholic refreshment, one (Kinly Stick) with no money to ring the bell at the bar for ordering and the other ('Heather Jock') with just enough to buy *'half a gill for the twae'*. Kinly rings the bell, but on the serving of the gill, 'Heather Jock', to Kinly's chagrin, scoffs the lot *'because that I was dry.'* Jock offers to sell the shirt from his back in order to allow them to ring the bar bell again. This was Easton's four-verse story, and in Grant's **(33)** turn of the century publication of the song, four verses remained. However, in his 1909 *The Book Of Hawick Songs And Verse*, James Edgar[42] gives a fifth verse, detailing an unsuccessful visit to Milmoe's pawn shop at 2 Orrock Place,[43] and this has remained. Adam Ingles **(55)** is unable to reveal whence came this verse, but there remains doubt about it being Easton's work. The characters portrayed were two of Hawick's less than eminent real Victorians – a 'bonny pair' by all accounts. Kinly[44] was one George Whillans – a renowned poacher, and 'Heather Jock' John Mitchell, a wrestler and general rough diamond, who is reputed to have walked from his home town, Hexham, to Hawick to find work. The 1871 Census reveals the former to be living at 1 Mid Row and the latter at 9 Kirk Wynd. Whillans is described as a 'wool frame work knitter' and Mitchell a 'woollen frame work knitter.' Mitchell appears to have degenerated into little more than a vagrant, collecting moss and sleeping rough, often on the heath – hence his *soubriquet*. The *Hawick Advertiser* (10/10/1874) carries a report of him being rescued, half submerged, from the Teviot, 'having been imbibing of his favourite beverage rather freely... it was only after considerable effort that his deliverers could arouse him to a state of semi-consciousness.' He died, aged 64, of tetanus in Jedburgh Jail some seven years later (7/12/1881). Whillans died, aged 62, three months earlier (11/9/1881), having fallen downstairs and sustained fatal internal injuries. The song probably predates 'Heather Jock''s descent into chronic oblivion by a year or two, perhaps between 1870 and 1872, but this is no more than speculation. Ingles[45] posits an unsupported theory that Mitchell had been in Australia (quite a feat at this time, if it is to be believed, with sailing ships being the only means of transport) and may have returned to Hawick singing or whistling the catchy sheep shearing song *Click Go The Shears*. Even there, in 1870, this was a new song, having been 'collected' in USA, some would say pinched, by an Australian professor of music called the Reverend Dr. Percy Jones. The song was never overtly religious but the words could be interpreted allegorically to evangelical advantage. It was a song of the American Civil War entitled *Ring The Bell, Watchman*, written in 1865 by Henry Clay Work (1832-1884). It relates the story of a watchman in a tower, about to ring the bell on receiving news of victory. If it reached Hawick by 1870 via popularisation in America and then in Australia, it was doing pretty well. It is remarkable, however, just how much of the 'skeleton' of Work's original song survives in *Kinly Stick*. Compare Work's *'High in the belfry the old sexton stands, Grasping the rope with his thin bony hands'* with *'In the big room at Barclay's the Auld Stick he stands, Grasping the bell rope with cold shaking hands'*. The Australian sheep shearers' version is *'Out on the board the old shearer stands, Grasping the shears in his long bony hands.'* Their chorus is *'Click go the shears boys, click, click, click'* while Work's original chorus reads, *'Ring the bell, watchman, Ring! Ring! Ring! Yes! Yes! The good news is now on the wing.'* In Hawick – *'Ring the bell, Kinly, ring, ring, ring! 'Heather Jock''s approaching, the good news to bring.'* The Australian version is a rollicking, joyous song and Work's original is also upbeat, rejoicing in *'glorious and blessèd tidings'*; neither presage the somewhat heavy chordal treatment given to it by Grant (**33**) or the rather elegiac version in Hawick Saxhorn Band's repertoire. Seeley's (**86**) arrangement in the 2001 anthology seeks to restore some gaiety to the song. Key: C Maj. Range: C-E$^|$.

61. Laidlaw, Robert H. (1872-1953)

Robert Henderson Laidlaw was born at 6 Slitrig Bank, Hawick on 24th July, 1872.[46] On leaving school he was apprenticed to the printing trade but, after a while, emigrated to America and worked as a printer in Boston. Returning to Hawick, he joined the *Hawick Express* under James Edgar, becoming his foreman printer. A man of considerable literary gifts and one who was fortunate to be in the employ of one of the Borders' most erudite newspaper editor/owners, he was encouraged to contribute his work to the newspaper – poems mainly, but he also contributed the weekly 'Betty Whutson' column, which drew on topical, social and historical events in the town to form an essay in the Hawick vernacular. Two of his poems were set to music and they will ensure his place in the Pantheon of Hawick song – *Auld Hawick, My Dreams* **(4)** and *Teviotdale* **(93)**. He also contributed papers to Hawick Archaeological Society. Laidlaw was an ardent churchman, connected with Hawick West Port Church, where he was Session Clerk for twenty five years and Sunday School superintendent. He was also a lay preacher whose services in churches in Hawick's rural hinterland were warmly appreciated. A Freemason, his connection was with Lodge St. James 424. Robert Laidlaw died, aged 80, at his home, 22 Beaconsfield Terrace, Hawick on 21st January, 1953 and was buried in Wellogate Cemetery.

62. Landles, Ian W. (b. 1952)

Ian William Landles was born in Edinburgh on 15th June, 1952. Educated at Hawick High School, he proceeded to Edinburgh University where, in 1974, he graduated MA with honours in History. Following teacher training at Moray House College of Education, Edinburgh, he returned to Hawick High School, where, in due course, he became Head of the History Department – a post he retained until his retirement in 2009. His interest in, and love for, his native town has been an all-consuming passion. He has been a relentless advocate of the Hawick 'mither tongue' – influenced, no doubt, by its effectiveness and verbal colour in his father's (William Landles **(63)**) poetry. He has himself dabbled in versifying, producing at least two fine Hawick songs – *Auld Hawick, Ma Border Hame* **(3)** and *My Teviot Valley* **(72)** and a plethora of song parodies for occasions when humour is of the essence. There are also shorter songs like *Hornshole* **(48)** written for one-man entertainments. His longer poem, *The Vertish Hill* and his moving poetical tribute to legendary rugby commentator, Bill McLaren, *The Man That Oo Ca' Bill*, together with his adaptation *Doon Oor Close And Up Oor Stair* reveal a creative mind of extraordinary versatility – a talent confirmed in his collaboration with Alan Brydon **(14)** in the creation of the highly successful musical play *A Reiver's Moon* in 2007 (and more songs). With Brydon, he is co-author of a book devoted to Border walks (*Walking In The Land Of The Reivers*) – another of his passions. Possessed of a sharp eye for detail in social interaction, he is an engaging and sought-after after-dinner speaker – a raconteur of wit and a master of irony. Perhaps this is most clearly exemplified in the three volumes he produced in the final decade of the twentieth century in collaboration with local photographer Derek Lunn, where his clever text complements some inspiring photography. These are *Honest Men And Bright-Eyed Daughters, Mair Honest Men ...,* and *Son Of Honest Men ... .* His musical facility has made him the most acceptable of pianists at St. Leonard's Hut at Common Riding time, though he is by no means limited to such occasions, stepping in when required at most functions. Ian Landles's commitment to Hawick has no boundaries. His contribution to the community of Hawick and its environs was recognised in 2004 when he was selected as Chief Guest for the Common Riding – a special honour since he was the first so chosen from within the town in recent times. Official civic recognition of his unstinting service to the community came in the Queen`s Birthday Honours List of 2013, when he was awarded the British Empire Medal (BEM). Apart from his pianistic contributions at 'the Hut' over more than two decades, he has held the presidencies of the 1514 Club (1991) and Hawick Callants' Club (2009), both awarding him honorary life membership. The Landles acrostic is today as much a part of the Callants' Club Dinner as were the pre-War essays of Tom Ker **(59)**. He is also a Mosstrooper and a member of the exclusive Anvil Crew. These clubs have all benefited from his counsel. His support of Hawick Archaeological Society is indicative of that same passion which has driven all his dealings in the 'grey auld toon'. He was its secretary for twenty five years, served as president, holds its honorary life membership and continues to be its major guiding influence. His influence has been felt throughout Hawick, not only in overtly Common Riding issues, but in aspects of its physical appearance – civic statuary, for example; he was a prime mover, with Ian Seeley **(86)**, in the creation and placement of the Adam Grant plaque at 2 High Street in 1999; also the James Thomson statue (2007) and the Bill McLaren bust in Wilton Park (2013). He is a director of the Bill McLaren Foundation and chairman of the Will H. Ogilvie Committee. In 2000, a *Hawick News* poll adjudged him Hawick's Citizen of the Year. Landles continues to disseminate his comprehensive knowledge of Hawick, its history, its culture, its language and its people through a series of night 'clesses' which have enjoyed lasting popularity. Indeed, what he doesn't know about Hawick is not worth knowing.

63. Landles, William (1912-1998)

William Landles (Willie, as he was affectionately known in Hawick) was born at 7 Sandbed, Hawick on 27th June, 1912. Educated at Buccleuch School then at Wilton School (which, at that time, took secondary pupils to the then statutory leaving age of fourteen) he followed in the footsteps of so many similarly gifted Teries and went into the hosiery industry, in his case, with Messrs. Turner & Rutherford, but soon switched to tweeds in the warehouse of Robert Noble & Co.'s Glebe Mills. His ability was recognised and he was promoted to the post of company secretary. Owing to amalgamations and rationalisation which became increasing post-War occurrences, he worked for a period with Roberts of Selkirk and Thorburn of Walkerburn. His final period of full-time work was a return to knitwear in Hawick with the firm of John Laing, Slitrig Crescent. He retired in 1977 but engaged in writing reports of Sheriff Court proceedings for *Hawick News*. This was his working background, but it was his remarkable literary skills in poetry and prose which marked him out from the crowd. He was a prolific contributor to newspapers (national and local) with over 400 of his poems published. He also contributed many exhaustively researched articles to the local press. His published collections of verse included *A Breath Frae The Hills*, *Gooseberry Fair*, *Penny Numbers* and *Turn O' The Year*. For over forty years, from 1953 he contributed to *Hawick News*, his *Thought For The Week*, an article combining original topical observations in prose and occasional verse with a personal message of Christianity. These essays were published under the pseudonym 'Quartus' and some were later published in booklet form as the *Quartus Notebooks*, namely *I To The Hills*, *All Good Gifts Around Us* and *Roving Commission*. His verse is seldom less than consistent in its discernment and quality. He never 'pads' for the sake of a rhyme, and every word, whether it be English or from his native vernacular vocabulary, is well chosen in its ability to strike a chord with the listener. The inspiration he drew from the history, tradition and inborn love of his home town and its environs is immediately evident in his *Hame Toun*, *The Exile's Return* and *Borthwick Water* **(13)**. The last of these was given a melody by Adam Ingles **(55)** and, in the 2001 song anthology, an accompaniment by Ian Seeley **(86)**. Willie Landles was never afraid to proclaim, without ostentation, a deeply held Christian faith and became a dedicated leader of the local Christian Brethren. Essentially a quiet but earnest man, he earned the respect of the respected Border writers of his generation, such as Will Ogilvie, Hugh MacDiarmid and Lavinia Derwent (better known to him, no doubt, as Betty Dodd). He was awarded the MBE in 1996. Willie Landles died, aged 86, at St. Margaret's Home, Bright Street, Hawick on 28th December, 1998 and was buried in Wellogate Cemetery.

64. Lassie That Works In The Mill, The

This attractive pseudo folk song is attributed to Walter Armstrong Peden **(78)** (1863-1954). The version of it given in the 2001 revised and enlarged edition of *The Hawick Songs – A Complete Collection (ed. Seeley)* is not the song as sung by Peden. Peden's melody consisted only of the first sixteen bars with repetition of same for the chorus. In the version presented, Henry Douglas **(22)**, a folk singer of some renown, has interpolated eight bars of 'new' material, giving the melody a temporary modulation at bar 24. It has to be conceded, at the expense of the purists, that this improves the song, bringing respite from the continuous repetition of the original binary (AB) melody by employing the more engaging ternary (ABA) form. It is always invidious to point out similarities to other compositions but whether by pure chance or by design, the first four bars of this new (B) section are note for note identical to the first phrase of the student song *Abdul, The Bulbul Ameer.*[47] Ian Seeley**(86)**, as editor, has provided a vamp accompaniment for the verse(s) but indulges the pianist with an attractive countermelody in the chorus. Following Walter Peden's death, the song was sung with some frequency by his sons, George (1913-1964) and John (Jock) (1913-1984). Key: F Maj. Range: C-D|.

65. Letham, James (b. 1954)

James George Anderson Letham, composer of *The Best O' A'*, was born at 40 Cairnhill Road, Airdrie on 15th May, 1954, Showing musical promise from an early age, he started taking piano lessons around the age of nine in Aberdeen. He was able to continue with these when his family moved to St. Andrews and his secondary education was at the town's Madras College which had a thriving music department under the leadership of the redoubtable Margaret Currie Affleck. (Ian Seeley **(86)** was one of her *protégés* just over a decade earlier). Jim also had lessons on French horn while at Madras College. From here he went on to study at the

Royal Scottish Academy of Music, Glasgow, gaining its graduate level diploma (Dip. Mus. Ed. RSAM) in 1975. Following teacher training at Jordanhill College, Glasgow, he was appointed to Galashiels Academy by Hawick's Brian Bonsor (at that time, Music Adviser for Borders Region). Bonsor recognised Letham's outstanding abilities and he was appointed Head of Music at Jedburgh Grammar School in 1981 before following Ian Seeley in a similar capacity at Hawick High School in 1997 – a post he held until his retirement in 2011. His input to both educational and social musical activity across the Border area has been enormous. He has been musical director for Hawick Amateur Operatic Society on four occasions – a task he has replicated for the Galashiels and Melrose Societies. He was also conductor of the Eildon Singers and the Borders Youth Orchestra, besides maintaining an ongoing commitment to Melrose Parish Church Choir. His work at Hawick High School was outstanding, especially in the sphere of musicals, which have inspired a significant number of his pupils to pursue careers in musical theatre. His affinity for the communities in which he has worked has produced some amazing results – notably in Hawick his community choir – Melody Makers, which also involved a measure of integration with his High School work. Jim Letham is an accomplished pianist and conductor who has also enjoyed success in composition. Since his retiral, he has been undertaking professional concert work and notably, locally, promoting the work of Hawick-born composer Sir John Blackwood McEwan (1868-1948). The mentoring and friendship of Brian Bonsor (1926-2011) (another outstanding Hawick-born musician) has had a profound effect on much of Jim Letham's work – much of it to the great benefit of Hawick.

66. Mackay, Neil (1928-1996)

Daniel (Neil) Mackay was born at 10 Slitrig Crescent, Hawick on 25th August, 1928, the house occupied by his grandfather, Richard Lynn, in his capacity as burgh foreman. He was the son of William Gibson Mackay, draper – an occupation that he would later follow. Educated at Hawick High School and the Royal High School, Edinburgh, where he was a boarder, he went on to serve with the Royal Signals in Ceylon (Sri Lanka). On his return, he took over the Hawick store in his father's business in Croft Road. In May, 1969, he was elected to the old Hawick Town Council to serve the ward of Burnfoot. He subsequently served as Hawick's Dean of Guild and as a County Councillor for Roxburghshire. He was a Justice of the Peace and was later to serve as Vice-Chairman of Roxburgh District Council until 1980. But it was his Burnfoot connection that produced, in 1970, his Hawick song – *Home By Burnfoot* **(47)**. Mackay was a keen amateur pianist and writer (he was the originator of the *Janus* column in the *Hawick News*). He was also influential in setting up the Town Twinning arrangement between Hawick and Bailleul and was sometime chairman of Hawick Chamber of Trade. His Masonic connection was with Lodge St. John 111. Neil Mackay died, aged 67, at his home, Glenfield, 5 Wilton Glebe, Hawick on 24th March, 1996 and was buried in Wilton Cemetery.

67. McCartney, Robert (1909-1996)

Robert McCartney's *A Song O' Hawick* **(89)** is steadily gaining recognition as one of the most sincere, yet understated triumphs of the 2001 song anthology. Robert was essentially a gentle man and that character shines through in this song. He was born at Wilton Dean on 27th May, 1909, but spent most of his early life in Myerslawgreen, attending first Drumlanrig School then Hawick High School where he was a Kennedy-Dechan gold medallist in 1924. An aptitude with figures saw him enter the local law practice of Thomas

Purdom & Son, where he specialised in accounting and taxation. Apart from his war service – most of it spent as a 'Desert Rat' with Montgomery's Eighth Army – his whole working life was with Purdom's. He was sometime treasurer of Hawick Liberal Club and enjoyed a long association with Hawick PSA Male Voice Choir (of which he was auditor). He was quietly interested in music. Never pretentious in any way, he derived great pleasure from playing the mouth organ. The last eight years of his life were spent at Buccleuch Rest Home. Robert McCartney died, aged 87, at Hawick Cottage Hospital on 12th November, 1996 and was laid to rest in Wellogate Cemetery.

68. Meda's Song

This is one of the two extant original songs from the Edwardian melodrama *The Gutterbludes*, with words by J.E.D. Murray **(70)** and music by Adam Grant **(33)**. The reason for this song's survival is that, like its fellow survivor, *Clinty's Song* **(18)**, Grant not only published it, but included it in his bound collections, entitled simply *Hawick Songs.* Grant had a good, but tragic, reason for publishing this song. He wished to dedicate it to the memory of his only daughter, Agnes Wight Hall Grant (Nan), who died, aged twenty five, after a very brief illness, on 13th April, 1912. The original front cover of *Meda's Song* carries the inscription 'IN MEMORIAM A.W.H.G.' Sometimes it is referred to as *The Song Of Meda,* which is the title Grant gives on the reverse front page of the song while retaining the shorter title for the cover. The song as it is sung today has achieved considerable popularity (despite lacking a chorus) and is altogether a much grander affair than its stage purpose originally demanded. In the play, it is sung in a snowbound cabin in the Canadian outback by a Hawick exile disguised (for reasons of detection) as an Indian scout – and one who is missing his belovèd Borderland. The song is sung unaccompanied or, at the producer's discretion, with the minimum of instrumental support (perhaps a solo fiddle or penny whistle on-stage). In his original publication, Grant provided a fairly simple chordal accompaniment in his preferred 'modified hymn tune' style, but Adam Ingles **(55)** dispensed with this completely in 1957, and paradoxically, at a time when anything Victorian was seen as *passé*, produced a pseudo-Victorian florid accompaniment. In 2001, Ian Seeley **(86)** restored a chordal accompaniment, albeit of more modern chord progression than the Edwardian original. The original key of the song was G Major. Ingles took it down by a tone. Key: F Maj. Range: C-D|.

69. Mosstrooper's Song, The

This stirring song (subtitled *Four Hunder Horsemen*) is the work of J.E.D. Murray (1858-1936) **(70)** and Adam N. McL. Colledge (1872-1965) **(19)**. Colledge was an avid horseman and it was inevitable that he should strike up a friendship with Murray. Colledge penned the music in 1928 and Adam Grant published the song in 1931 – his final Hawick song publication, because, by this time, his business was in decline and, two years later, it was advertised for sale as a going concern on the front page of the *Hawick Express* of 19th January, 1933. (In fact, there were no takers and Grant's son managed, with difficulty, to keep it going for a further five years, but new Grant publications were at an end). Murray's words are broad Hawick. Although Colledge produced a fine melody, his original piano accompaniment was stiff and lacking the flexibility that the words seemed to suggest. The harmonic progressions also seemed ill-chosen. This is one song that Adam Ingles **(55)** definitely did improve in 1957, and Ian Seeley **(86)** made some further adjustments to the accompaniment in 2001. The effect of the accompaniment now is that the song has the atmosphere of the ride and a sense of direction that, in the original, was lacking. The song has always been popular, though, like Tom Ker's **(59)** songs, it has differently worded 'choruses' for each verse. The song, since it was printed on the back of their 1937 Dinner menu, has been adopted by the Ancient Order of Mosstroopers as their club song. Key: E♭ Maj. Range: B♭₁-E♭¹.

70. Murray, J.E.D. (1858-1936)

Clinty's Song **(18)**, *Meda's Song* **(68)**, *The Wail Of Flodden* **(97)**, *Invocation* **(57)** and *The Mosstrooper's Song* **(69)** – all songs with lyrics by J.E.D. Murray. John Edward Dodd Murray was born at 57 High Street, Hawick on 10th August, 1858,[48] a son of John Murray, plumber. As John Murray's (senior) business (and family) grew, the family moved to 2 Union Street where his son–in-law, James Brand ran his own school – Teviot Grove Academy (commonly known in Hawick as Brand's School). It is thought, however that J.E.D. may have attended Buccleuch School (forerunner of the present Hawick High School). Whatever, when he left school, he was apprenticed to John Wield, druggist of 48 High Street. His health damaged by the chemicals with which he worked, he left Hawick for Gateshead where he worked as a grocer. We next hear of him in Liverpool, selling medical supplies to the White Star Line shipping company. Following this, he was in insurance, in which, we are informed, the business of collecting and selling was aided by the ability to ride a horse, so nurturing a life long passion for these animals. Murray, in these early years, seems to have been a rolling stone, for his next move was into photography with a John McKean of Leith. He returned to Hawick in 1886, his wandering days over, and set up as a 'Photographic Artist' at a site in Bridge Street at its corner with Croft Road. Photography would occupy the remainder of his working life. But Murray had other gifts – poetry, prose, elocution, anything in fact, to do with the theatre (he did make-up for Hawick Amateur Operatic Society up to the year before his death in 1936) and horsemanship which drew him inextricably into Hawick Common Riding. His return to Hawick was co-incidental with an increasing civic pride and the building of a magnificent new Town Hall. In 1887, a Ceremonial Committee was set up to regulate and formalise certain aspects of The Common Riding. J.E.D. Murray had a significant influence on that committee and, increasingly, his Common Riding poetry was gaining him a voice in the development of the festival. James Edgar invited Murray to write the introductory article to his *Hawick Songs And Recitations* of 1892. He was on the way to becoming the personification of the Common Riding, being elected Cornet in 1890 and serving as Acting Father no less than four times (1901, 1905, 1912 and 1925). He was a founder member of Hawick Callants' Club in 1903 and was instrumental in the founding of the Ancient Order of Mosstroopers in 1920. Four of the songs mentioned above originate in Murray's dramatic creations. He was a keen and capable amateur playwright who wrote sketches for special occasions e.g. *The Caddie's Ghost* for Hawick Golf Club (1894), *The Witch O' The Wisp Hill* for Hawick Queen Victoria's Jubilee Nurse Endowment Scheme (1901), *Kirsty O' Cocklaw Castle* for a Hawick Saxhorn Band Grand Bazaar (1904) and, in 1912, *Turning Back the Clock* for another fund raising bazaar, this time for Hawick and Wilton Cricket Club. For all of these, his friend and contemporary, Adam Grant **(33)** provided incidental music. His *piece de résistance*, was, of course, *The Gutterbludes* of 1905/06. 1914 saw him as Pageant Master (co-ordinator/producer) for *The Hawick Quater-Centenary Historical Pageant*, to which he also contributed – giving us *The Wail Of Flodden* and *Invocation.* His position as the doyen of Hawick Common Riding was unique and his reputation as one of Hawick's most venerated citizens unassailable, and yet he found time for other things – painting, outdoor pursuits like camping and trekking, writing a book about the latter – *Over The Rolling Stones By One Of Them* – in 1895. James Edward Dodd Murray was truly 'a man of many parts.' He died, aged 78, at 43 North Bridge Street, Hawick on 27th November, 1936 and was buried in Wellogate Cemetery.

71. My Borderland

This song, composed by Albert Budge **(15)** to words by David Johnston **(58)**, was one of a handful of 'new' songs which kept the flame of local song-writing alive following the Second World War. *My Borderland,* Adam Ingles's **(55)** *Auld Hawick, Where I Was Born* **(5)** and *Auld Hawick, My Dreams* **(4)**, together with Frank Simpson's **(87)** *Teviotdale* **(93)** all appeared between 1950 and 1955. Although the last of these is rarely heard, *My Borderland* has held its own with the first two others mentioned. It uses, arguably, David Johnston's best set of words from the composer's point of view, allowing him to 'wax lyrical'. It is a rewarding song to sing, not only for its wide range but for its natural flow of expression in climax and anti-climax, and it benefits from having a good chorus. For most ordinary singers, the high F$^|$ is probably an F too far, and perhaps this is a song which, in future anthologies, needs to come down a tone. The song was written in 1950. *My Borderland* is a song well-suited to the female voice. Indeed, it was first heard on 7th June, 1950 in a Braemar (Innes, Henderson & Co.) factory broadcast, sung by Miss. Ina Wintrope, a member of Hawick Amateur Operatic Society. *The Hawick Express* (31/5/1950) gives the details – 'Mr. David Johnston... has written the words for a new song entitled 'My Borderland', which has been set to music by Mr. Albert V. Budge, and it is to be included in the numbers broadcast over the factory service on the 'nicht afore the morn.' The singer will be Miss. Ina Wintrope.' The song was sung at the Overseas Nights of 1951 and 1952 by Mrs. Margaret (Peggy) Helm. The *Hawick Express* (29/10/1952) reported its publication by a London music publisher at the end of October, 1952, priced 2/-. Key: F Maj. Range: C-F$^|$.

72. My Teviot Valley

My Teviot Valley has not had the same amount of exposure as Ian Landles's **(62)** *Auld Hawick, Ma Border Hame* **(3)**, but it has the potential to be a favourite. It is altogether a more lyrical song and it doesn't have a chorus. It is one of a number of good songs written over the last two decades which could do with a champion, notwithstanding the writer/composer's own occasional performances of it. The song was first performed on 27th March, 2004 on top of Hawick Moat by the author when he was leading a walking party as part of Reivers' Weekend that year! Landles later brought this song to Ian Seeley for arrangement, but Seeley was incapacitated by treatment for a serious illness and his version of the accompaniment was not completed until a year later. The song is well written, musically, and its lyrics bespeak Landles's love for his provenance with fitting eloquence. It would be inconceivable for it not to appear in any future anthology. Key: E♭ Maj. Range: B♭₁-E♭¹.

73. Old Mill Town

If David Finnie **(29)** never wrote another song, this one would ensure his place in the Pantheon of the Hawick genre. Its success has been quite extraordinary, but why shouldn't it be? It is the work of a man entirely at ease with his chosen style – a style which owes much to the pseudo folk song genre which had an immense following in USA post 1960 (with artists like Joan Baez and Bob Dylan building on the legacies of such as Huddie Ledbetter, Woodie Guthrie and Pete Seeger). It is an immensely pervasive style which informs the work of other present day composers in Hawick, such as, for example, Alan Brydon **(14)** and George Goodfellow **(31)**. *Old Mill Town* is a subtle, understated, but compelling song. The song is quietly passionate and the name Hawick is never explicitly mentioned, but all its iconic symbolism is there. If ever a song reflected the personality of its composer, this is it – articulate, concise, quietly earnest yet understated and modest. Finnie doesn't command attention by bawling; instead, he soothes and beguiles the listener, inviting them to join in the chorus. The song, inspired by the composer's view of Hawick as he returned to the town from the north, via the A7, was written in 2001 and scored for voice and guitar – (*'I'm looking down on this old mill town, making my way back home...'*). Ian Seeley **(86)** subsequently transcribed its guitar accompaniment for the piano. Key: C Maj. Range: A₁-C¹.

74. Old Song, The

This is the oldest Hawick song, believed to have been written some time in the two decades straddling the turn of the Eighteenth and Nineteenth Centuries. It would be easier to date the song more accurately if a date of death for Arthur Balbirnie **(6)** were known, but extensive trawling of old parish records and grave inscriptions in Hawick has failed, so far, to reveal this. It has been suggested that the song was added to over a period of years (cf. also *Kinly Stick* **(60)** in which a verse is believed to have been added at a later date). The verse which poses the dating problem is verse 8 - '*But, by the by, I'd maist forgot it, // The Mycelaw Green, we'll just be at it; // There we'll get a guid cauld caulker // Frae a man that is nae Quaker.*' This verse refers to the minister of the West United Presbyterian Church – the 'Green Kirk' – Andrew Rodgie (1777-1860), who was liberal with alcoholic refreshment to Common riders. But Rodgie wasn't inducted into the Hawick church until August, 1807, which would have made the song date, at the very earliest, later than the 1808 Common Riding. Otherwise, it had been supposed that the song was written c. 1800. But this is all conjecture. In 1800, assuming he was still alive, Balbirnie would have been sixty five. Balbirnie's song describes the Common Riding of his day. The first three verses are given to the historical context of the Common Riding and the following ten deal with the socio-geographic aspect – in other words, what happens where. Today, *The Old Song* is sung annually from the steps of Drumlanrig's Tower after the Cornet's Breakfast on Common Riding (Friday) morning. The tune is, of course, *Teribus* **(92)**, also known as *The Air Eternal*, but, it has to be said, Balbirnie's verses, at places, are ill-fitted to it. *The Old Song* was overtaken as the traditional Common Riding song by James Hogg's *The Colour* **(20)**, following its publication in 1819.

75. Oor Ain Auld Toon

This song made its debut at the Colour Bussing of 1903 when it was sung by Hawick's distinguished tenor, John Bell.[49] The words are by Thomas Caldwell**(16)** and the music by Adam Grant **(33)**. *Oor Ain Auld Toon*, on the original printed copy, carries the dedication, 'To all Hawick Callants in Exile', making it a *sine qua non* for Exiles' or Overseas Night programmes. All the necessary ingredients are there – evocative verses and an excellent chorus. Of all Grant's piano accompaniments, this is the one in which he demonstrates variety, abandoning his *penchant* for hymn tune-like chordal progression throughout in favour of a mixture of supportive single bass notes and rhythmic chords with chordal passages. This variety is refreshing and brings to the song a leanness and vigour. It is a song which may be very effective when sung by the female voice. (Out of seventeen programme appearances at Colour Bussing ceremonies between 1903 and 1939, it was performed by women on eight occasions). A very satisfying song for both singer and accompanist. Key: G Maj. Range: D-E♭.

76. Oor Bonnie Border Toon

On Friday, 11th June, 1897 the *Hawick News* reported – 'Today we publish a poem he (Robert Hunter **(51)**) has produced entitled 'Oor Bonnie Border Toon' which, if one of our local musicians would kindly compose a tune for it, would make an admirable Common Riding song.' Such an exhortation was clearly irresistible to the young Francis George Scott (1880-1958) **(84)**. Almost five years elapsed and, on 4th June, 1902 the *Hawick Advertiser* noted, 'OOR BONNIE BORDER TOON – Messrs. W. & J. Kennedy have issued a new Hawick song which is sure to have a popular sale... Like Mr. Hunter's other poetical pieces, his song has a fine poetical ring about it, while Mr. Scott has wedded it to a fine tune, so 'Oor Bonnie Border Toon' should e'er long be one of our most popular local songs.' The following week, it was sung at the Colour Bussing by Ex-Cornet James Sutherland. Given its popularity today, it is perplexing to find that it was not sung again at such a gathering until after the Second World War – which gives credence to the theory that certain songs really need a champion. This is an exhilarating, if challenging, song for both singer and accompanist and it has an emotive, almost reverential, chorus. In the original publication, there was a four-bar interlude between the verses and a four-bar piano coda at the end of the song which Scott agreed to omit for the 1957 anthology. The four-bar introduction is now played between each verse, although Hawick Saxhorn Band still plays the original interlude in George Guy's 1935 arrangement, *Memoirs of Hawick*. Key: B♭Maj. Range: B♭₁-F¹.

77. Pawkie Paiterson

There has always been a deal of uncertainty about this song and its origins – the words are whose? Where did the melody originate? John ('Soapy') Ballantyne **(7)** has been given the credit for what appears to be a parody of an older Northumbrian song, since there seems little doubt that he sang it at functions at which he entertained. John W. Kennedy, (Hawick Archaeological Society Transactions, 1915) claims that 'J. C. Goodfellow thinks it an imitation of a Northumbrian ballad, viz. *Robin Spraggan's Auld Grey Mare,*' the verses for which originated in that county`s Felton district (some eight miles south of Alnwick and fifty miles south east of Hawick). There are twelve verses in the Felton version[50] in which the characterisation and sentiment are so similar to that found in Hawick`s *Pawkie* as to banish any doubt that this is indeed the provenance of our song; but the tune is different, giving rise to the notion that Ballantyne, or another, adopted the very Northumbrian pipe-sounding tune that we use today. There was also a suggestion that *Pawkie* was written by Dr. John Douglas (1788-1861), whose sterling work in the Hawick cholera outbreak attracted much local approbation, but who was also a *literatus*. Frank Hogg **(45)**, in a paper to the same society (23/12/1873) reckons that the Hawick song 'was written about sixty years ago' (c. 1813), but the Felton original is probably some thirty to forty years older still. There is less doubt about the characters, or 'worthies' portrayed. Rob Paterson of 9 Loan has been immortalised as Pawkie; Margaret (Peggy) Duncan lived in Kirk Wynd and could not be deemed a beauty; Nellie Harkness (wife of Tom Harkness, a labourer) was Pawkie's niece (*'...and cries, 'O Godsake, uncle, the yaud's among the corn!'*). The others are Rob Young, blacksmith/farrier 'o' the Back Raw', dry-stane dyker, 'Stonie' Stewart and, of course, the 'minister o' Wilton' (in the original, as sung to Frank Hogg by James Hardie, '*the priest o' Wilton*'). Hogg was not over-enamoured with the melody, noting, 'the tune is not very rich in music, I must say, but when sung in the old Hawick style, it is thoroughly enjoyable.' Most Teries would concur. *Pawkie Paiterson* is one of only three Hawick songs to be written in compound time (the other two are *The Best O' A'* **(9)** and *Hawick Stands Alone* **(42)**). The sung melody differs in its last four bars from that played by the Cornet's Band (Drums and Fifes). In the latter, the last four bars of the melody are identical to the first four. This is also the version given in William Laidlaw`s *Drumlanrig Quadrilles,* published by W. & J. Kennedy 'in commemoration of the Laying of the Memorial Stone of the New Municipal Buildings, August, 1885.' What is sung today is probably

Adam Grant's **(33)** transcription of local singers' 'wont and usage.' *Pawkie Paiterson* has been a favourite at Colour Bussing ceremonies since these occasions were formalised in 1887. Key: B♭ Maj. Range: A₁ -D♭.

78. Peden, Walter A. (1863-1954)

Walter Armstrong Peden was born at 19 Hall Street, Galashiels on 23rd July, 1863. Of Hawick stock, he established himself there (Hawick) as a butcher. He was quietly dedicated to the affairs of Hawick and its Common Riding. An avid horseman and cyclist, he was also an office bearer in Masonic Lodge St. James 424 and a member of Buccleuch Bowling Club. The Pedens had a long association with East Bank (now Trinity) Church and Walter was one of its ruling elders. *The Lassie That Works In The Mill* **(64)**, attributed to Walter Peden, must be one of the most unaffected yet engaging songs to be inspired by the everyday, non-ambitious life of a mill girl – simple joy and acceptance of one's lot in life. After Walter Peden's death, the song was sung with frequency by his sons George (1913-1964) and John (Jock) (1913-1984). Walter Peden died in his 91st year on 20th March, 1954 at 3 Buccleuch Terrace, Hawick and was laid to rest in Wellogate Cemetery.

79. Queen O' The Auld Scottish Border, The

This is the third of Ian Seeley's **(86)** five Hawick songs and probably the most accessible. It is certainly the one which has been most performed. It was written early in 1995 and dedicated to local historian, raconteur and wit Ian Landles **(62)** in recognition of all the encouragement given by him to the composer in his assimilation of all things Hawick. It is certainly a pleasant song on the ear, but some of Seeley's versification (particularly at the end of the first verse) could give McGonagall a run for his money. The song was published by the composer's friend, J. Elliot Renwick (1936-2006) at his firm – Buccleuch Printers – in 1995. Key: F Maj. Range: C-E♭.

80. Return From Hornshole

This song by Alan Brydon **(14)** is about as far removed from his *The Bonnie Banner Blue* **(10)** as can be imagined. The song was first performed at the 1514 Club's 'Hawick Sings' concert in May, 2011 by the composer's daughter, Cheryl. The song, being in the minor key, has a haunting wistfulness, yet it is in no way passive. The rising sequences at the beginning of each verse bring to it an insistent quality which gives the song drive. Ian Seeley **(86)** was asked by the composer to provide a piano accompaniment in line with his conceptions of mood, chordal structure, etc. It might be said that Seeley has pushed his musical academicism further in this song than in any other of his arrangements (the accompanist has to be able to play the piano to a high standard of proficiency) but he has provided something which enhances the atmosphere already created by Brydon. This is, in some ways, a specialist, or art, song, but this shouldn't deter its progress; there are currently in Hawick many capable young singers with whom this style is familiar. Key: A Min. Range: E$_{\flat}$-A (but may be sung one octave higher).

81. Robson, William I. (1853-1891)

William Inglis Robson's progression from blacksmith to professor of music has to be a story of inspiration. He was born in 1853, probably at Appletreehall, just outside Hawick, where his father, James Robson, ran a blacksmith's business.[51] William, on his Marriage Certificate (31/12/1875) gives his occupation as 'Blacksmith Journeyman' living at 12 Wilton Crescent, but within fifteen years he had become a distinguished teacher of music in Glasgow schools, had written the music for *Hawick Among The Hills* **(38)** (1887) and *Up Wi' The Banner* **(96)** (1888), been awarded the Fellowship of the Tonic Sol-fa College (FTSC) (1890) after a gruelling musical examination covering advanced harmony, double counterpoint, orchestration and musicology, and had been appointed a professor at the School of Music for Scotland in connection with the Glasgow Atheneum (later to become the Royal Scottish Academy of Music). During this journey to professionalism he began using his mother's maiden name – Inglis – as a middle name. He never intended to create a double-barrelled surname because his son, William Scott Robson (author of *The Story of Hawick* and *Hawick Place Names*) was named after his wife (Nancy Scott).The details of his own early musical education have yet to be revealed but, in 1881, he was advertising as an instructor for the Tonic Sol-fa College from his home at 1 Laing Terrace while working as a frame smith (mill engineer) during the day. To all intents and purposes, his success stemmed from his espousal of John Curwen's[52] 'new notation' method (Sol-fa) of teaching musical literacy and singing to the masses. In 1882, he was leader of St. Mary's choir when he won the Curwen Scholarship of the Tonic Sol-fa College in London, where he completed the course successfully, gaining honours in composition and voice training and also passed the examination for admission to the London Musical Composition Club. At the end of 1882, he became a Graduate of the Tonic Sol-fa College (GTSC) and was engaged by the Synod of U.P. Churches as a teacher of music. 1883 saw him appointed leader of psalmody (out of twenty seven candidates) at Queen Anne Street U.P. Church, Dunfermline and in 1884 he was teaching in schools run by Glasgow and Govan School Boards – a task visited with such success, that in1890 he was invited to join the staff of the newly-established School of Music for Scotland as detailed above as 'Professor of Harmony, Singing, etc. and both notations of music.' (*Hawick News* 16/8/1890). During the last seven years of his life, he was choirmaster of Free St. George's Church, Glasgow. William Inglis Robson died, aged 38, after a protracted illness, at Rosebank Terrace, Cambuslang on 13th November, 1891. His remains were brought back to Hawick and interred in Wilton Cemetery.

82. Rosenberg, M

This was the pseudonym used by Adam Grant **(33)** around the turn of the nineteenth and twentieth centuries. The *Hawick News* (17/6/1898), for example, informs us of the 'new song entitled *Hawick*, the words by J. L. Hercus, and the music by M. Rosenberg.' Ker's **(59)** *I Like Auld Hawick The Best* (1900) carried a similar attribution, but later prints (same design *motifs*, same format) carried the good Scots name Grant. Grant appears to have believed that a Germanic name would be more beneficial to sales, and it seems to have been a fad in vogue at that time. Although Grant was still selling copies with the Rosenberg attribution up to the First World War, he had, even by the early years of the new century, reverted to using his own name – and the time was fast approaching when anything faintly suggesting German inspiration would be shunned. Even the British Royal Family would have to change its name.[53]

83. Rutherford, John (1838-1914)

The composer of *The Border Queen* **(12)**, John Rutherford, was born in the west end of Hawick (probably Village)[54] in 1838. From the censuses of 1841 and 1851, he appears to have been orphaned at a very early age. In 1851, he was described as 'lodger, pauper and scholar', aged thirteen, living in Kirk Wynd under the roof of an Irish widow, Bridget Durkin. The Irish connection, and hence, his eventual religious persuasion, was a powerful influence in his early years. He became a shoemaker to trade, working in the firm of R. & W. Burnet of the Howegate, and it is as such that he is recorded in the 1861 Census, again as a lodger (married to an Irishwoman) with an Irish family. He was, apparently, the possessor of a fine baritone voice and was a leading musician in the choir of the local Roman Catholic Church. He emigrated to Sydney, Australia in 1884 in order to assist a widowed sister and her daughter in the management of an hotel. This was the Middlesburgh Hotel, from whence emanated a report of a

'Hawick Night', sent to the *Hawick Advertiser* (25/7/1885) noting 'of which Mr. John Rutherford, late with Mr. Burnet, Howegate, is the landlord.' The letter detailed Rutherford singing two songs in the evening's musical programme – *I Like Auld Hawick* and *Pawkie Paiterson* – but no mention of *The Border Queen*! He became an eminent member of the Sydney Scottish Borderers Association and remained committed to his home town – so much so that he made two return visits to Hawick (1892 and 1901) and was planning a further return for the 1914 'Home-Coming' when, in retirement at Petersham (a suburb of Sydney) New South Wales, he was taken ill. He died, aged 76, on 21st June, 1914 and was buried in the Roman Catholic sector of the massive Rookwood Necropolis, Sydney.

84. Scott, Francis G. (1880-1958)

Generally regarded as the greatest Scottish composer of songs, and composer of *Oor Bonnie Border Toon* **(76)**, Francis George Scott was born on 25th January, 1880 at 6 Oliver Crescent, Hawick, the son of a supplier of mill engineering parts. Though his specific early musical education is unclear, he was educated at Brand's School (Teviot Grove Academy) in Union Street, Hawick, from which he went to Edinburgh University to pursue, in the first instance, a general MA degree. As a result of a dispute, he did not complete his studies there but, at that time, was still able to become a teacher. He taught at Drumlanrig School, Langholm Academy and Dunoon. While at Langholm, he taught Christopher Grieve – who was to become, as Hugh MacDiarmid, Scotland's greatest poet of the twentieth century. Their mutual inspiration and friendship was to be lifelong, (Scott also dabbled in poetry) but also, while at Langholm, he studied for the degree of Bachelor of Music (BMus) which was conferred upon him at Durham in September, 1909. He subsequently studied composition under Jean Roger-Ducasse at the Paris Conservatoire and in 1925 was appointed Lecturer in Music at Jordanhill Teachers' Training College, Glasgow, in which post he remained until his retirement in 1946. Francis George Scott was possessed of a formidable original musical talent. His Hawick song is light years away from what he was doing in the 1920s and 1930s in the *avant garde* of vocal music. His problem was, and always has been, that his artistic gifts were not fully recognised by the British (basically, English) musical establishment, if at all. He was a formidable pianist (an 'ordinary' pianist will struggle to do justice to Scott's settings of Robert Burns, William Soutar, William Dunbar, Hugh MacDiarmid and many others – he wrote over 300 songs). Some of his songs are fiendishly difficult for even the most accomplished performers. In the years between the two World Wars, with his cousin – the artist William Johnston, and poet Hugh MacDiarmid, he sought to bring about a Scottish Renaissance of the arts, condemning the subservience of Scottish culture to English values. This was co-incidental with the general intellectual dissatisfaction which gave birth to the National Party of Scotland in 1928 (the Scottish authors Neil Gunn and Eric Linklater were also heavily involved in this fore-runner of the SNP). Scott was a complex and sometimes difficult man to deal with, not one ready to compromise without cast iron reasons for so doing. Adam Ingles **(55)** reported finding him 'difficult' and 'intractable' when he made his approaches regarding the inclusion of *Oor Bonnie Border Toon* **(76)** in the 1957 song anthology. In that very same year, Glasgow University conferred the honorary degree of Doctor of Laws (LLD) on Francis George Scott. It might have been thought that an honorary doctorate in Music (DMus) would have been more appropriate; but then, Hawick's man – a man of independent mind – never was one of the establishment, and to that extent, the LLD was the greater honour. Francis George Scott died, aged 78, on 6th November, 1958 in a nursing home at 1055 Great Western Road, Glasgow. His remains were brought back to Hawick for interment in Wellogate Cemetery.

85. Scott, Iain H. (b. 1968)

A great great nephew of Francis George Scott **(84)** and youngest son of Hawick Honorary Provost Frank T. Scott, Iain Hunter Scott was born in Edinburgh on 30th October, 1968 and was educated at Hawick High School. The main thrust of school music at that time still had as its basis Class Singing, which, in spite of Scott's undoubted musical gifts, held no attraction or chance of inspiration for him, and he was not alone. His interest was largely inspired by contemporary popular, folk and pseudo folk music together with a growing interest in ever-developing music technology, but the guitar would be the foundation of his musical creativity. On leaving school he was apprenticed as a joiner and carpenter in the Hawick firm of Brydons and attended Borders College, the facilities team of which he joined in 1992. This led in 2004 to a lectureship in construction at the college. With his friend David Chapman, he became, in 2001, co-founder of the highly successful self-proclaimed 'Folk 'n' Roll' band 'Scocha' which has played all over the world and produced five albums, several singles, a live DVD and a video recording in partnership with Borders Heritage, playing the music for the television production *The Clans.* In 2006, he recorded and produced Hawick Callants' Club's CD *Teviotdale in Song and Poetry.* In 2013, following in the footsteps of his father and grandfather (R.E. Scott), he became President of Hawick Archaeological Society. He has given much time to making recordings of local performers for posterity. He is a Mosstrooper and an avid supporter of the Common Riding and all things Hawick. His approach to music is utterly professional and nothing but the highest standards will satisfy him. He has performed his own music to Thomson`s **(94)** *The Auld Mid Raw* and Hogg`s **(46)** *Carterhaugh Ba',* but these are not yet in score. The arrangement of Alan Brydon's *The Bonnie Banner Blue* **(10)** was entrusted to Iain Scott, and the piano scoring of his intentions realised by Ian Seeley **(86)**.

86. Seeley, Ian W. (b. 1942)

Ian William Seeley was born in St. Andrews, Fife on 22nd December, 1942, the third child in a family of seven, and educated at the town's Madras College. He was a latecomer to music, starting to learn piano aged eleven, but with encouragement from the school's distinguished rector, Dr. John Thompson and his formidable Head of Music, Margaret Currie Affleck, he proceeded to the Royal Scottish Academy of Music, Glasgow and Trinity College of Music, London, following this with teacher training at Dundee College of Education and emerging as a qualified teacher in April 1965 with a job in prospect at Inverness Royal Academy. He was briefly Master of Music at Iona Abbey before commencing his teaching career. While in London, he was fortunate to have as his mentor the distinguished London conductor and composer Charles Proctor, who encouraged him to study for the Bachelor of Music degree. London University conferred that degree (BMus) upon him in 1973. He was to follow this up with study at Edinburgh University which awarded him the degree of Master of Education (MEd) in 1982. An MA degree in education followed from the Open University in 1991. He has always thrived on 'projects'. These were projects which enhanced his own learning (he had already gained the music diplomas of the three main London colleges – LTCL (1964), ARCM (1978) and LRAM (1979)), so his teaching career was based upon sound practical and theoretical musical knowledge. Seeley arrived in Hawick in April, 1970 to take up post as Head of Music at Hawick High School, having held similar positions in Kirkwall Grammar School (1966-1968) and Lockerbie Academy (1968-1970). His assimilation into Hawick, largely because of the nature of his profession, was swift; he was organist of Trinity Church within a week of arrival – a position which he held for the following twelve years. The first Teri house he ever was in was that of Adam Ingles **(55)** at Rosebank – and he and Ingles maintained a warm friendship until the older man's death in 1991. Perhaps it was prophetic, because, at that stage, Seeley never believed he would be involved with the Common Riding, let alone becoming a Mosstrooper or editing the Callants' Club song anthology. He busied himself in his school work, presenting Gilbert and Sullivan comic operas, carol festivals and the like. He was also involved, sporadically over many years, with Hawick Amateur Operatic Society, writing the definitive history of the Society, *On With The Show*, for its centenary in 2010. For this he was awarded the National Operatic and Dramatic Association's (NODA) Medal of Commendation. A Rotarian for many years until illness forced his resignation, he was president of Hawick Rotary Club in 1998 and was awarded Rotary's highest accolade – a Paul Harris Fellowship – in 2003. He was variously conductor of Hawick P.S.A. Male Voice Choir and musical director for the operatic society and served on the committees of Hawick Saxhorn Band and Hawick Archaeological Society, of which, for a few years, he was also a trustee. Although always a supporter of Hawick Common Riding, it was only with the declining health of Adam Ingles that he was invited to take on a more practical role from 1987. He became pianist, in turn, to the 1514 Club, the Ancient Order of Mosstroopers, Hawick Callants' Club, the Ex-Cornets and Ex-Acting Fathers Association and, from 2002, the Colour Bussing. In 2001 he was invited to be musical editor of the Callants' Club's revision and enlarging of *The Hawick Songs – A Complete Collection*. The club awarded him honorary life membership in recognition of his efforts and, in 2008, the Ancient Order of Mosstroopers adjudged him Mosstrooper of the Year, recognising, similarly, his contribution to the town's culture. (He followed Cornet Alan Wear to Mosspaul in 1996). Seeley, like Adam Ingles before him, has been liberal with his talents, playing for myriad associations and clubs in the town and its hinterland and occasionally speaking at their functions. Apart from his five Hawick songs (*Callant's Song* **(17)**, *Where Teviot*

Rins **(100)**, *The Queen O' The Auld Scottish Border* **(79)**, *Hawick Reivers* **(41)** and *Songs Of Teviotdale* **(90)**) he is a nationally published composer of organ and choral church music, whose work has received critical acclaim in various periodicals. He has written some 115 poems, some of which have been published in *St. Andrews In Focus* and the *Aberdeen Leopard* magazines.

87. Simpson, Frank (1888-1964)

Francis (Frank) Simpson was born at 10 Trinity Street, Hawick, the son of mill foreman, Thomas B. Simpson, on 22nd July, 1888. Little is known about his early training, but his song *Teviotdale* **(93)** demonstrates a level of musical sophistication that, in Hawick song at least, is barely matched by any of his contemporaries. He was a church organist at Newcastleton and later at Minto but had a fairly low musical profile in Hawick, apart from giving music lessons at his home at 4 Earl Street. Frank Simpson died, aged 77, at Dingleton Hospital, Melrose on 1st May, 1964 and was buried in Wilton Cemetery.

88. Smith, Janet (1908-1974)

Jenny Ferguson was born at 14 Princes Street, Stirling on 11th September, 1908. Educated at Stirling High School, she went on to primary teacher training at Dundee Teachers' Training College (1928-1930) where, in addition to the normal qualification, she gained an extra endorsement permitting her to teach music. Her teaching career began in 1930 at Yetholm on the Scottish Border. She married the local baker, Scottish rugby internationalist Robert T. Smith in 1932, and they moved to Manchester for a period before returning in the late 1930s to Hawick where he took over the old established Bridge Street bakery of W. & R. Johnstone, turning it into a first class business. Widowed in 1958, Mrs. Smith taught in Drumlanrig St. Cuthbert's Primary School, Hawick from 1964 to 1971. She wrote the music for *Hurrah! For The Cornet* **(52)** in 1968, the words being devised by her Primary 5 class. She entered the 'Song for Burnfoot' competition in 1970 with a song entitled *The Jewel In The Crown*, which also featured some of her school pupils, but was unsuccessful, Neil Mackay's **(66)** *Home By Burnfoot* **(47)** winning the day. Following her departure from Drumlanrig School, Mrs. Smith remarried, becoming Mrs. Doward, but it was to be a union of short duration. She died three years later in Hawick Cottage Hospital on 20th July, 1974 and was interred in Wilton Cemetery.

89. Song O' Hawick, A

In the summer of 1990 Ian Seeley **(86)** was visited at his home by a carer from Hawick's Buccleuch Rest Home. Mrs. Vivienne Anderson brought with her an audio cassette of one of her charges, Robert McCartney **(67)** singing a song which he had made up that was 'going round in his head'; would Mr. Seeley kindly listen to it and, if possible, transcribe it and write a piano part for it. McCartney also had his words written on a scrap of paper, but the third verse was no more than a sketch. Seeley transcribed the two complete verses and retained the third sketched verse in the expectation that he would visit the composer to discuss tidying up loose ends. This never happened. In the meantime, he despatched what he had done to McCartney. A local ladies' singing group – *Quintessence* – visited the home and Robert McCartney passed them a copy of the newly finished manuscript. Taken by the song's simple charm, they sang it at many of their performances so that when the Callants' Club song book revision committee met to ponder possible new inclusions in their 2001 anthology, McCartney's song had already made some kind of impression in the town. The committee did feel, however, that McCartney's sketched third verse should be 'enhanced' and included. This was done by suggestions from within the committee's membership. The song benefits from an unaffected simple charm which is also reflected in

Seeley's arrangement. It also has the advantage of having a very wistful, though understated chorus. The song has, already, one or two champions who clearly enjoy singing it. Key: G Maj. Range: D-D$^|$.

90. Songs Of Teviotdale

This is the last of Ian Seeley's **(86)** five Hawick songs. It was written at the beginning of May, 1996 specifically for the Hawick-born professional tenor Elliot Goldie who, in his late school years, the composer had tutored. Goldie had recorded the first four songs and this song was a token of the composer's thanks. Goldie's rendition of *Songs Of Teviotdale* is included in Hawick Callants' Club's CD *Hawick and Teviotdale in Song and Poetry.* As to the song itself, Seeley had clearly been inspired by the new experience, for him, of riding in the Border hills and was soon to become a Mosstrooper; 'the Hawick experience' had claimed him. Musically, he was acutely aware that his last song required a very different, 'plusher' treatment to that of his previous essays. (The five songs are all very different in style). Key: E♭ Maj. Range: B♭$_|$-E♭$^|$.

91. Taylor, Joshua J. H. (1831-1910)

Joshua Joseph Henry Taylor hailed from the Huddersfield district. He arrived in Hawick in 1884 to take up a position as a worsted designer with Messrs. Blenkhorn, Richardson, tweed manufacturers. (Blenkhorn was also a native of Yorkshire, belonging to Thirsk). By the time he retired, he was mill manager for the firm, but he could have followed a different, though perhaps less secure, career in music. He was an exceptionally gifted musician as his music for *The Banner Blue* **(8)** in its original form demonstrates. But this shows only one side of Taylor; his *forte* was choral church music. His anthems like *Blow Ye The Trumpets In Zion*, *Come, Ye Children*, *Rend Your Hearts* and a full Church of England Service enjoyed wide currency in their time. These were all composed before he came to Hawick and were to be heard in places like York Minster, Durham Cathedral and St. Paul's Cathedral in London. *Rend Your Hearts* appeared on the first concert programme of the newly-formed Hawick Amateur Orchestral Society on 16th March, 1891 under the baton of Walter Fiddes-Wilson.[55] The *Hawick Advertiser* (20/3/1891) observed it to be 'for solo and quartette...displaying beautiful and conceptive writing.' The same newspaper reported some eight months later (6/11/1891) a new *Te Deum* by Taylor, sung in Wilton Church on 31st October, 1891 showing 'great scholarship'. His last anthem – *If, With All Your Hearts* – was also composed in Hawick. He had begun playing the organ aged eighteen and was fascinated by its capabilities. When Wilton Church introduced its first pipe organ in 1886, he served for a year as honorary organist. In spite of his undoubted talent, he was, according to Wilton's minister, John Rudge Wilson, 'a modest, retiring man.'[56] Joshua Taylor died, aged 79, at his home – 2 Wilton Hill, Hawick on 16th April, 1910 and was buried in Wilton Cemetery.

92. Teribus

Teribus, today, is synonymous with *The Colour* **(20)** by James Hogg **(46)** and could be called the Common Riding Song proper. Technically speaking, however, *Teribus* is the melody adopted by Hawick (because it was around these parts long before Balbirnie **(6)** and Hogg **(46)** employed it as the vehicle for their respective lyrics). There is a record of 'The original set of Teribuss as played by Walter Ballentine, Town piper in 1777.'[57] This tune is clearly a forerunner of the tune in use today, but even today's tune is subject to minor alteration depending upon who plays it and where it is played. The version played by the drums and fifes is different to that sung at functions, and both have slight melodic variation from that printed by Adam Grant **(33)** in his compiled *Hawick Songs*. The first appearance of *Teribus* in print is reckoned to be at the beginning of the nineteenth century in *A Second Collection of Strathspeys, Reels, etc., by John Pringle*, published in Edinburgh, and 'printed for the author and to be had at his lodgings No.16 Rose Street.'[58] The melody is believed to have originated in Northumbria and some commentators have remarked on its striking resemblance to that of the Tyneside song *Bobby Shaftoe*, but much is conjecture, save to say that the melody and the battle-cry of 'Teribus!', for that matter, are rooted in antiquity, giving rise to James Hogg's reported reply on being asked about its age – 'Its air's eternal!' – in modern parlance, 'It's aye been!' Hence, *Teribus* is frequently referred to as *The Air Eternal*. The etymology of the word *Teribus* is discussed in entry **20** as is the existence of another tune of the same name, played by pipers throughout the country, but bearing no resemblance to Hawick`s tune. Hogg's poem *The Colour* is, in most Teri minds, *Teribus*. In 1898, the Hawick born lawyer and poet, Robert S. Craig (1867-1921)[59] produced an alternative set of words to *Teribus* in his poem '1514',[60] but Hogg's words, apparently, are unassailable – '*Teribus ye Teriodin! Sons of heroes slain at Flodden, Imitating Border bowmen, Aye defend your Rights and Common*' vanquished to obscurity '*Teribus ye Teriodin! By our sires who fell at Flodden, Muster swift and rouse the river! Strike for Hawick, Auld Hawick for ever!*'

93. Teviotdale

This exquisitely well-written song deserves to be heard more often, but the odds are stacked against it; it is a 'true singer's' song, perceived to be just a bit too sophisticated, and it doesn't have a chorus. Robert Laidlaw's **(61)** words first appeared, without attribution, in the *Hawick Express* of 20th September, 1934. The poem was reprinted by the same newspaper (7/6/1950) in its *Poet's Corner* beside a report of its debut as a song with music by Frank Simpson **(87)**. *Teviotdale* was given its first performance at the Glasgow Hawick Association's Common Riding Night on 2nd June,

1950 in the Ca'doro Restaurant, Union Street, Glasgow in the presence of Cornet Tom Crosby and his lass. The singer was Mrs. Margaret Turnbull (*née* Scott), a niece of the Hawick-born composer Francis George Scott **(84)**. Margaret Turnbull`s soprano voice was probably well suited to the song's original key of D Major, but the suggestion to the composer that he should lower the song by two tones for publication (to which he agreed) undoubtedly made it more accessible to a wider range of singers. Key: B♭ Maj. Range: B♭₁-F¹.

94. Thomson, James (1827-1888)

Not a Hawick man, and not to be confused with Ednam's James Thomson (1700-1748) – of *Rule, Britannia* renown, but revered in Hawick as 'yin o' oor ain', James Thomson was born in Bowden, Roxburghshire on 4th July, 1827, becoming a cabinet maker and wood turner to trade and serving his apprenticeship in Selkirk. Thomson moved to Hawick to follow his trade and lived in the town for about forty years, most of them spent in parlous health. He was locked into poetry from a very early age and, as a boy, would carry a tattered copy of the Kilmarnock edition of Burns' poems under his plaid. Small wonder then that he would become president of Hawick Burns Club. His output of poetry was by no means copious, but he left a number of real nuggets in his *oeuvre.* Of real importance to the world is his *The Star O' Robbie Burns* with music by James Booth (1850-1919),[61] a touring music-hall musician he is believed to have met when the latter was performing at the Hawick Exchange. Of local importance are the two sets of magnificent Hawick verses he penned, one set within two years of his death (*Up Wi' The Banner* **(96)**). His earlier *tour de force* is, of course, *The Border Queen* **(12)**, the lines of which were significant in the choice of location for William Landles's (artist/sculptor cousin of William Landles **(63)**) impressive statue of Thomson – '*Where Slitrig dances doon* *the glen to join the Teviot waters*' – facing the confluence of these two rivers and, appropriately, flanked by Hawick Burns Club. Thomson's other two significant, though less high profile, Hawick pieces are *Our Hawick Volunteers* **(43)** and *The Auld Mid Raw*, which was set to music by Iain H. Scott **(85)** and performed with the renowned local folk rock band 'Scocha'. Other gems like *The Mither Tongue*, *The Wee Croodlin' Doo* and *Hairst* crop up from time to time, but it is his share in the two big Hawick songs and, of course, his Burns world anthem, which have brought him added immortality. Thomson was a member of the Mystic Craft, his affiliation being with Lodge St. James 424, in which he also filled the office of Bard. In 1870, he was persuaded by friends to publish a volume of his works under the title of *Doric Lays and Lyrics*, which met with such success that a second, enlarged edition was called for in 1884. This comprises fifty six poems and includes, for the first time, *The Border Queen* **(12)**. *Up Wi` The Banner* **(96)** is a 'one-off' and does not appear even in posthumous editions. In the last year of his life, the Masonic brotherhood gave him much assistance in his tribulations; it was they who arranged for his hospital care as the end approached. Thomson died in Hawick Cottage Hospital, aged 61, on 21st December, 1888 and was buried in Wellogate Cemetery, where, on 3rd June, 1899 a handsome obelisk was unveiled in his memory. The James Thomson Memorial Bridge over the River Teviot was opened in 2005. He will not be forgotten in Hawick.

95. Up Wi' Auld Hawick

This is surely Hawick's convivial anthem: it is history, geography, philosophy and 'wha's like us' all rolled into one – with an important extra – the action in the chorus, which endorses the sentiments of the verses and arms are interlinked over one's neighbour's shoulders. The first intimation of the issue of the song was in the *Hawick News* of 9th May, 1902. The original printed copy carries on the cover the dedication '*Written and Composed for Mr. John Bell*', but it was sung at the ensuing Colour Bussing for the first time, not by him, but by Mr. Colin Jardine. Bell sang it at the following three such ceremonies, after which it was performed by others (Bell left Hawick in 1909 and spent the rest of his life in Edinburgh). The song is one of two Hawick songs in which there is a change of time signature for the chorus (the other is *I Like Auld Hawick The Best* **(54)**). The change is from 4/4 to 3/4 - from a march to a waltz. (In the other named song, the change is from 3/4 to 4/4 – the reverse, in fact). And what a waltz it is! Caldwell's **(16)** words are ebullient, bullish and just so reflective of the confidence of the early Edwardian years. Grant **(33)** has come up with a tune that could grace any seaside promenade or garden fête – an atmosphere that Hawick Saxhorn Bandmaster, Robert Rimmer captured exquisitely in his arrangement of the song in his *Hawick Songs* medley (c. 1913). Again, as in so many pieces that are popular, the listening/singing public seem determined to alter the melody through 'wont and usage' by singing the uppermost three accompaniment notes for the last note of the verse, rather than sustain the high D♭ as written. Similarly, there is a predilection for singing '*O'er the Borders SHE'S Queen*' rather than Caldwell's intended '*O'er the Borders THE Queen.*' The Hawick public have indeed taken ownership of this song. Key: G Maj. Range: D-D♭.

96. Up Wi' The Banner

The words of this song were written some twenty months before their author, James Thomson, died in December, 1888. They were dedicated and presented on the eve of the 1887 Common Riding to Cornet Tom Scott (a brother of the founder of the knitwear firm, Peter Scott) – and they were sung at that year's Colour Bussing by Robert Telfer Paterson to the tune of *Hail To The Chief.* (This tune has been adopted as the official Presidential Anthem of the USA, but is itself a parody on Sir Walter Scott's *Lady Of The Lake* Canto XIX, the melody for which was composed by the English theatre composer, James Sanderson (c. 1769-1841)). In late 1887, the tune used today was composed. The *only* song, as far as Teries are concerned, employing Thomson's words, is William Inglis Robson's **(81)** setting, which was heralded by an advertisement in the *Hawick Express* of 11th February, 1888. The song was published by Messrs. Paterson, Sons & Co. and subsequently by W. & J. Kennedy of the Sandbed, Hawick. Robert Telfer Paterson (no relation to the publishers) performed it at the Colour Bussing that year and it has never looked back. It is second (some would say joint second) with the *The Border Queen* **(12)**) only to *Teribus* in public affection and has been sung at almost every Colour Bussing ceremony since 1888. Robson clearly intended his piece to be ceremonial. He introduces the song with an eight-bar fanfare (which is seldom played in its entirety today – in fact, one feels it has a bar missing and that the first three bars should really be four). What follows is, by any standards, a first class triumphal march. Within the chorus are two two-bar interpolations (allusions to *Teribus*). These, today, are often omitted, but when they are included, there is frequent argument as to whether they should be played at double speed or at the same speed as the rest of the song. The correct speed is given by Robson in the original printed copy where he clearly states *tempo primo (trumpets)* first time and *tutti* (everybody) second time; in other words, the speed of the introductory fanfare – no argument. Interesting also, with reference to the original words, is that Thomson actually wrote '*Boast Scotland, boast of the deeds of your fathers.*' To some Teries, no doubt, especially at Common Riding time, Hawick *is* Scotland! The original key was G Major but it was taken down a tone by Adam Ingles **(55)** in 1957. Key: F Maj. Range: C-D|.

97. Wail Of Flodden, The

This evocative song comes from Part V (*Fatal Flodden*) of the 1914 Hawick Quater-Centenary Historical Pageant, with words from the pen of J.E.D. Murray **(70)** and music by Adam Grant **(33)**. It was, in fact, written for Miss. Jessie Easton Murray who would, four months later, become Grant's daughter-in-law.[62] Jessie Murray (1890-1976), a machinist with the Peter Scott company, was a noted contralto in the town and she was given the part of Ailie, a widowed victim of Flodden, in the pageant. The minor tonality of the song renders it replete with the aura of disaster and an empty future. Grant succeeds in this song because he is able to use his preferred style of chordal accompaniment to maximum effect. He published the song in the summer of 1915, the *Hawick Express* (2/7/1915) referring to its words as 'beautiful and pathetic.' George Guy includes it in his band arrangement, *Memoirs of Hawick* (1935). Unfortunately, since the nineteen nineties, Grant's original melody has been all but supplanted by a bastardised 'pseudo-folk' version of the song, perpetrated by John Wright, a shepherd folksinger, now deceased, but with a considerable local following. *The Wail Of Flodden* heard most often today, sadly, is 'the song *not* written by Adam Grant.' Key: E Min. Range: B|-D|.

98. We'll Follow Oor Cornet Roon'

This song is today the club song of the 1514 Club, with words by David Johnston **(58)** and music by Adam Ingles **(55)** who dedicated his setting to the Club in 1975. The song's details – 'Music by Adam Ingles, etc.' – are given in the *Hawick Express* (6/6/1975). David Johnston most certainly was not thinking of the 1514 Club when, on 2nd May, 1951 the *Hawick Express* printed in full *We'll Follow Oor Cornet Roon'* – more than a decade before the club's formation. Johnston's poem is in no way pretentious: it is simply a Common Riding poem and it tells succinctly what Hawick Common Riding is about – commemoration, reassertion, community, camaraderie and friendship. The tune is not Ingles's most refined work, but it is definitely fit for purpose, is tuneful, has drive and a simple, inclusive chorus. It works. Key: F Maj. Range: B♭₁-Dᶦ.

99. Where Slitrig And Teviot Meet

This song, by Tom Ker **(59)**, has probably gathered more dust than any other in two centuries plus of Hawick song writing. Apart from the composer's own renditions of it at the functions of the old Teviotdale Amateur Bicycle Club in the final decade of the nineteenth century and at Callants' Club functions (for example, that reported by the *Hawick Express* (31/3/1905)[63] in the Tower Hotel), it was largely forgotten until Adam Rutherford Grant **(34)** resuscitated it from bits of manuscript left by his father and promoted its performance by Mr. William Oliver at the Callants' Club Congratulatory Smoker to the Cornet in the Tower Hotel on 18ᵗʰ May, 1949. It is doubtful as to whether it has been heard since at any function of import. The reasons are not hard to find. Although the melody of the song is pleasant, Ker's words are, at best, banal, and at worst, space-filling doggerel. It is noteworthy that though it was found among his music after his death, Adam Ingles could not bring himself to include it in the 1957 anthology. The decision to include it in the 2001 anthology was more about preserving a piece of song history than expanding the repertoire. It is also significant that Adam Grant senior **(33)** showed no inclination to publish the song in spite, no doubt, of hearing it on several occasions at the bicycle club of which he had been captain. Ian Seeley **(86)** provided an attractive accompaniment for the song in 2001, but the unpalatable truth is that the song is flawed. Key: G Maj. Range: B₁-Eᶦ.

100. Where Teviot Rins

This song, Ian Seeley's **(86)** second of five Hawick songs, was written for his wife, Alison, at the end of August, 1994. It has been performed at several Hawick Nights by the lady for whom it was written, but has yet to find a wider patronage. The song is almost minimalist in construction – the singer does the work and the accompaniment provides a few well-chosen chords with judicious use of silence (rests) in the part below the words. The four-bar piano introduction is slightly fuller, as is the coda, but not much. This sparseness of approach gives the song a healthy leanness – the air gets in – and brings to it a certain delicacy and poignancy – *Where Teviot rins, I long to be.*' The words and music, like most of Seeley's essays, were conceived simultaneously. Key: E♭ Maj. Range: B♭₁-E♭¹.

CHRONOLOGY

c. 1800	Old Song, The
c. 1813	Pawkie Paiterson
1819	Colour, The (Teribus)
1860	Hawick Volunteers
c. 1870	Anvil Crew, The
c. 1872	Kinly Stick
1874	Bonnie Teviotdale
c. 1876	I Like Auld Hawick
c. 1885	Border Queen, The
1887	Hawick Among The Hills *
1888	Up Wi' The Banner
c. 1890	Fairest Spot O' A', The
c. 1890	Where Slitrig And Teviot Meet
1892	Banner Blue, The
1898	Hawick
1900	I Like Auld Hawick The Best
1902	Oor Bonnie Border Toon
1902	Up Wi' Auld Hawick
1903	Oor Ain Auld Toon
1905	Meda's Song
1905	Clinty's Song
1914	Wail Of Flodden, The
1914	Invocation
c. 1925	Lassie That Works In The Mill, The
1928	Mosstrooper's Song, The

1932	Exile's Dream, The
c. 1947	Hawick Callant, The
1950	Auld Hawick, Where I Was Born
1950	Teviotdale
1950	My Borderland
1955	Auld Hawick, My Dreams
1968	Hurrah! For The Cornet
1970	Home By Burnfoot
1975	We'll Follow Oor Cornet Roon'
c. 1975	Borthwick Water
1990	Song O' Hawick, A
1994	Callant's Song
1994	Where Teviot Rins
1995	Queen O' The Auld Scottish Border, The
1995	Hawick Reivers
1996	Songs Of Teviotdale
1996	Auld Hawick, Ma Border Hame
1996	Hawick Stands Alone
2000	Hawick Lasses 1514
2001	Old Mill Town
2004	My Teviot Valley
2005	Bonnie Banner Blue, The
2007	And We Ride
2008	Hornshole
2011	Best O' A', The
2011	Return From Hornshole
	* Disputed – perhaps 1889 – see notes

GLOSSARY

academic degrees –   MA – Master of Arts
MEd – Master of Education
BMus – Bachelor of Music
DMus – Doctor of Music
LLB – Bachelor of Laws
LLD – Doctor of Laws.

arpeggio – a 'spread` or broken chord, the individual notes of the
chord heard one after the other
(harp-like *arpa* – a harp).

binary – two-fold compositional form – a first section (A) and a
second, contrasting section (B).

cadence – a phrase ending.

chorale – Lutheran Germanic harmonised hymn tune of measured pace
and characterised by pauses at the phrase endings.

coda – a composed ending or tail piece usually with allusions to
previous themes in a 'tying up' process.

codetta – (*It.* little tail) short, or less important coda.

con furore – with fury (with enthusiasm).

counterpoint – the weaving together of independent melodies.

FSA Scot. – Fellow of the Society of Antiquaries of Scotland.

modal – referring to the use of the Mediaeval and early Christian
church modes which were the forerunners of the present day
major and minor tonalities. Sometimes referred to (wrongly)
as 'old minor'.

modulation – key change in the course of a piece.

music diplomas –
ALCM – Associate of London College of Music
LLCM – Licentiate of London College of Music.
LTSC – Licentiate of Tonic Sol-fa College.
GTSC – Graduate of Tonic Sol-fa College.
FTSC – Fellow of Tonic Sol-fa College.
ATCL – Associate of Trinity College, London.
LTCL – Licentiate of Trinity College, London.
ARCM – Associate of Royal College of Music
LRAM – Licentiate of Royal Academy of Music.
ARCO – Associate of Royal College of Organists.
FRCO – Fellow of Royal College of Organists.
DipMusEd RSAM – Diploma in Musical Education of Royal
Scottish Academy of Music.

recitando – declamatory in style.

RIBA –Royal Institute of British Architects.

seqence – a repetition in succession of a musical pattern which can
be melodic (i.e. in the tune) or harmonic (in the underlying
chordal structure).

soli – a number of soloists performing within the same piece – plural
of solo.

song pitch ranges – ₁ indicates below Middle C. ᴵ indicates above the B
above Middle C.

strophic – using the same music for each verse of a song.

symphony – any purely instrumental passage, e.g. the piano
introduction to a song – a coda or interlude.

ternary – three-fold compositional form – two contrasting sections
(AB) with a return to the first section (ABA).

turn – a melodic embellishment on a printed note – played the printed
note, the note above, the printed note, the note below, and the
printed note in quick succession – written ~ above the printed
note.

unison – without harmonisation – all 'as one' – e.g. bare octaves or, in
a choir, everyone singing the melody.

vaudeville – musical comedy style – music hall style.

NOTES & SOURCES

1. Murray, Robert – Hawick Songs and Song Writers (3rd Edn.) pp. 36, 37 – W. & J. Kennedy, Hawick 1897.

2. Ingles, Adam L. – Notes and Comments on the Songs of Hawick, p. 16 – Hawick Archaeological Society 1992.

3. Hawick Express – 31/3/1905 p. 3.

4. Hawick Express & Advertiser – 13/12/1918.

5. See 2 – p. 14.

6. Hawick Express – 3/5/1950.

7. See 1 – p. 27. The main problem with Murray's book is that, for him, song and poetry are synonymous; music and composers, apparently, are of little consequence, yet, by the time of his book`s publication, Hawick already had specially composed music for, for example, *The Banner Blue, Hawick Among The Hills, Up Wi' The Banner* and *I Like Auld Hawick.* When he comments on Balbirnie`s song, is Murray tacitly acknowledging that it is the earliest known Hawick song *with music*? (The Rev. Robert Cunningham (c.1668-1772) had written a poem – *Ode To Hawick* – as early as 1710, which would indicate that laudatory verse for Hawick and its history is considerably older than *The Old Song*).

8. Hawick Advertiser – 6/10/1905, p. 5.

9. Hawick Songs and Recitations – commentary by J.E.D. Murray, p. 8 – James Edgar pub., Hawick, 1892.

10. The Hawick Songs – A Complete Collection – ed. Ian W. Seeley – Hawick Callants' Club, 2001.

11. Stewart, Andy (1933-1993) – Scottish stage artiste in the Harry Lauder tradition who invariably ended his songs (whatever their sentiment) on an ostentatious high note.

12. The Hawick Songs – A Complete Collection – arr. Adam L. Ingles – Hawick Callants' Club, 1957.

13. Rimmer, Robert (1863-1934), a native of Southport, was Hawick Saxhorn Bandmaster 1905-1914. His *Hawick Songs* (c.1913) band medley (arrangement) covers the well-known Hawick songs such as appeared in Adam Grant`s compilations, including *Up Wi' The Banner, Pawkie Paiterson, The Border Queen, Oor Ain Auld Toon, I Like Auld Hawick The Best, Kinly Stick, Up Wi` Auld Hawick* and *Teribus.*

14. See 2 – p.5. The date of 1880 seems too early for a Grant-published Hawick song. Grant only arrived in Hawick in November, 1878, aged 19, and was barely established in the town in 1880, although he had moved into shared shop premises at 2 High Street in 1879. The only known Grant publication from his time at this venue is his *Branxholme Waltz* for piano. All other extant publications emanated from 10 Bridge Street, to which he moved in 1885. The published arrangement of Rutherford`s *The Border Queen* is by Grant and proclaimed so on the copy.

15. Simpson, David B., FRCO (1886-1941) – Born in Kilmarnock and reared in Dundee, he came to Hawick in 1920 to be organist at St. George's Church, this having been gifted a new pipe organ by Peter Scott (knitwear manufacturer) that year. He quickly established himself as a private music teacher capable of taking gifted students right up to diploma level. He was also conductor of Hawick Choral Society until it folded with the coming of the Second World War. He died, aged 54, in 1941 and was buried in Wellogate Cemetery, Hawick.

16. Hawick Advertiser – 4/12/1908, p. 4.

17. Reinle, Dr. K.E.R. – Dr. Reinle was a native of Lucerne, Switzerland. A graduate of Basel University, he arrived in Hawick in 1894 and became organist of Hawick Parish Church until 1901. He took private pupils for piano and singing and struck up a friendship with Dr. Barrie, J.E.D. Murray, Adam Grant and a number of other prominent men in Hawick at the turn of the Nineteenth and Twentieth Centuries. He was still in Hawick in 1905.

18. Dumbreck, Euphemia Ritchie – elder daughter of the composer of *I Like Auld Hawick*, is listed in the 1861 Census as being governess to the children of Walter Wilson, manufacturer, of Orchard House on the Cavers estate, four years before the establishment of Teviotside House school in Hawick. She died, aged 80, at 41 Drummond Place, Edinburgh on 22nd July, 1915 and was buried in the Old Burial Ground, St. Cuthbert`s, Edinburgh. Perhaps her position with the Wilsons indicated a need for the formal schooling of the offspring of a new social class in Hawick – the self-made men, or *nouveaux riches.*

19. Hawick Advertiser – 14/1/1865 – front page advertisement.

20. See 1 – pp. 57, 58.

21. The Anvil Crew is a select body of Hawick gentlemen who meet for their own dinner and entertainment on Common Riding (Friday) Evening. Their title is taken from Easton's song, their origin stemming from a group of men who could not get into the official Cornet's Dinner on that evening and so set up one of their own. An essential feature of the evening is its reference to 'nautical' aspects – e.g. the 'bus taking the party to Denholm (where the function is held at 'The Fox and Hounds' inn) is referred to as the boat and the chair- man is the Captain. Songs are sung and toasts very like those at the Cornet's Dinner are given.

22. Gotterson, Matthew – In 2000, when the new Hawick song anthology was mooted, no-one in Hawick seemed to have a clue as to the identity of this man. Birth and Death Register searches produced nothing and after much consideration and calculation, Ian Seeley and historian Ian Landles came to the mistaken conclusion that Gotterson must be a pseudonym of J.E.D. Murray. Consequently, the dates assigned to 'Gotterson' in 'The Hawick Songs – A Complete Collection 2001' are wrong. Seeley discovered by chance, in 2013, that Gotterson was, in fact, James Smail (1828-1905) and this was confirmed by data held by the Royal Bank of Scotland.

23. Grant, Adam – A fuller account of Grant's life can be found in Ian W. Seeley's article in Hawick Archaeological Society's Transactions 1997 – 'Adam Grant and the Hawick Songs.' Subsequent research, however, has revealed that Grant played for the Common Riding for 41 successive years, not the fifty as stated in this article. Seeley lifted this information from another writer whose assertion could not be documented. There is ample evidence, however, that Grant played sporadically for many Hawick functions from shortly after his arrival in the town.

24. Guy, George E. (1877-1956) was Hawick Saxhorn Bandmaster 1932-1945. His arrangement of Hawick pieces for brass band (they are not all songs) – *Memoirs Of Hawick* – was first performed 31/5/1935. It comprises thirteen numbers suitably arranged and linked – viz. 1. *Hawick*; 2. *The Lasses O' Hawick* (Howieson); 3. *The Song Of Meda*; 4a. *Gibbie's Dance* (polka); 4b. *Hobbie's Song* (both from *The Witch O' The Wisp Hill*); 5. *Oor Bonnie Border Toon*; 6. *The Wail Of Flodden*; 7. *The Anvil Crew*; 8. *John Patterson's Mare Rides Foremost*; 9. *Bonnie Teviotdale*; 10. *Clinty's Song*; 11. *The Mosstrooper's Song*; 12. *Teribus*; 13. *Finale* (Guy). The work was written in celebration of The Silver Jubilee of King George V.

25. Hawick News – 13/11/1908, p. 3.

26. Watson, Professor George – in Hawick Archaeological Society Transactions 13/3/1917, p. 3.

27. *Hawick Among The Hills* – There is some disputation about the year of Inglis Robson's setting. The Hawick Advertiser (8/6/1889) claims it 'was set to music specially for this occasion (The Colour Bussing) by Mr. Robson.' Mrs. John Smith (née Annie Cowan), reminiscing, somewhat confusedly, in the Hawick Express (17/6/1927, p. 3), about *Up Wi' The Banner* writes; ' Up Wi' The Banner' was sung by Mr. Robert Paterson at the 1887 Colour Bussing when, I believe, the words were sung to the.....melody of 'Hail To The Chief.' Mr. William Robson composed his haunting setting in time for the Common Riding of the ensuing year, and I am the proud possessor of the first copy sold. It was bought from the hands of the author when he called at our house in Silver Street (on Auld Clinty's Rock). Bussing, but had to withdraw on the death of her mother-in-law, Mrs. Smith but, she writes, 'Miss. Nellie Anderson took my place and sang the song from my copy.' The problem is that Miss. Anderson did not sing at all at the 1888 ceremony, but she did sing *Hawick Among The Hills* at the 1887 ceremony (at which Mr. R. T. Paterson also sang *Scotland Yet!* – the tune of which had previously been used for *Hawick Among The Hills*). It seems highly unlikely that the same tune would be used twice for different words on the same occasion. Mrs. Smith did, indeed, sing *Up Wi' The Banner*, but at the 1889 ceremony, when there was no sign of Nellie Anderson. It seems plausible, therefore, that it was *Hawick Among The Hills* that Mrs, Smith was given in February, 1887. The song was sung to Robson's tune by a Miss. McGregor at the 1889 Colour Bussing.

28. Reid, John G. (1721-1807) – General in the Hanoverian army. Fought at Culloden. Composer, flautist, Alumnus of Edinburgh University which received over £50,000 in his will, specifically to establish a Chair of Music and purchase books, instruments, concert rooms, etc. making it the envy of similar establishments throughout the world.

29. Hercus, James L. – There is a problem with Hercus's birth date. His Death Certificate (1885) gives his age as 39, which would mean a birth year of 1846 or 1847 (if he was in his 39th year). The Kirkwall Censuses of 1851 and 1861 claim that he was 2 and 12 respectively, giving a birth year of 1849, and both describe him as 'scholar' At 2? On his Marriage Certificate (31/12/1868) he gives his age as 21. This gives a year of birth as 1847, which has been accepted here.

30. Hercus, James L. – Songs of the Borderland and Other Verses – pp. 137, 138 J & J. H. Rutherford, Kelso & William Peace & Son, Kirkwall 1888.

31. Robson, W.S. FSA Scot. (1884-1950) – Hawick Place Names – p. 42 John Murray Hood, Hawick 1947. William Scott Robson was the son of the composer of *Up Wi' The Banner*, William Inglis Robson.

32. Scott, James - He *may* be James Scott, b. c. 1794 in Cavers Parish – a stocking maker on the Loan in 1841, Orrock Place in 1851 and at 9 Howegate in 1861.

33. Hogg, James – Both the plaque on the wall at 14 Loan and the refurbished stone in Wilton Old Churchyard give the wrong date of death (18/10/1838) for Hogg. The correct date was given by the Kelso Chronicle of 9th November, 1838, p. 6, col. 3 – 'Died at Hawick, on the 3d instant, James Hogg ... the author of the well-known 'Hawick Common Riding Song' ... has taken the place of all the olden songs on the same subject, and is exceedingly popular.' The Hawick old parish record concurs with the Kelso newspaper.

34. Opportunity Knocks – A 1970s Independent Television (ITV) talent-spotting show, with audience reaction gauged by the 'clapometer' – a crude recording of the intensity of applause hosted by presenter Hughie Green.

35. Hunter, James Y. – Biographical Sketch of the Poet (Robert Hunter) by his Son, Hawick Archaeological Society Transactions 1936.

36. Smith, James Dryden RIBA – A Hawick Miscellany – paper read to Hawick Archaeological Society – 18/12/1966 avers – 'It was a preparatory school for the children of parents who were of a certain standing in the town; Sir Thomas Henderson was one of the pupils who at a tender age had attended and could in later years recall pleasant memories of happy days there ... After the death of Mrs Dumbreck the family resident-associations with Hawick were terminated in 1885 when the Misses. Dumbreck retired to Colinton, Edinburgh.' (James Dryden Smith (1888-1968) was the son of Annie Cowan Smith – see note 27 – and the brother of Elliot Cowan Smith (1891-1917) – champion of the Hawick vernacular).

37. Paterson, Robert Telfer (1866-1907) – One of the finest basses of his time, a member of St. Cuthbert's Episcopal Church Choir and a frequent singer at Colour Bussing ceremonies and other Common Riding functions, he was responsible for the 'launching' of *Up Wi' The Banner* (1888), *Hawick* (1898) and *I Like Auld Hawick The Best* (1900).

38. Hawick Express – 18/5/1955, p. 5 – What! Change The Songs? – This report reveals the extent of the unease created by Adam Ingles's proposals. Ex-Cornet Bonsor – 'No-one has any right to interfere with another man's songs.' (He had heard that they had been 'altered in tune as well as in key'). Ex-Cornet Nuttall, of the Callants' Club song review committee had heard local singers sing the songs and they had been 'far from satisfied with the book as it was then.' Ex-Cornet Landles – 'We only granted the use of the copyright on the understanding that only the key of the songs would be altered.' What they got was well removed from their 'line in the sand' and demonstrates just how persuasive and manipulative Ingles was in his determination to bring about change. An editor carries enormous responsibilities. In this case, Ingles was performing a balancing act. Many of the songs were clogged with Victorian musical conventions in spite of their undoubted melodic attributes. The task he set himself was to save the songs from themselves, but such an exercise is always fraught, a mixture of gains and losses being the end result.

39. Ingles, Adam L. – Notes and Comments on the Songs of Hawick – p.7 – Hawick Archaeological Society 1992.

40. Ibid. – p. 19.

41. The location is behind the present 'Stag's Head' bar and was traditionally referred to as 'The Hole in the Wa'. See 2 – p. 9.

42. Edgar, James – The Book of Hawick Songs and Verse (Second Edition) – p. 8 – James Edgar, Hawick 1909.

43. The Milmoes were of Irish extraction. An advertisement in the Hawick Advertiser 4/11/1871 states - 'H. J. Milmoe gives the highest price for Ladies' and Gentlemen's LEFT OFF WEARING APPAREL & c. Letters punctually attended to – 2 Orrock Place.' ('*Then through the Sandbed the pair they did go, Streicht to the pawnshop that's kept by Milmoe;*'). Hugh Joseph Milmoe died at 5 Baker Street (which seems to have been the family home, as his younger brother and sister both died there) 11/5/ 1885 aged 65 and was buried in Wellogate Cemetery. His brother Patrick followed him 10/2/1886 and his sister Bridget 7/7/1899. Their Death Certificates describe them as 'brokers'.

44. Murray, Robert Murray – Hawick Characters; Second Series – p. 28 – James Edgar, Hawick 1914 Murray writes – 'George Whillans, like many of his townsmen, had a nickname – his was The Kinly Stick, being the name he gave to an old flint gun, with which he used to go a-poaching before the days of netting.' An out and out rogue, he was charged, in 1875, with murdering his wife, but was found not guilty. Whillans is buried in Wellogate Cemetery.

45. Ingles, Adam L. – See 2, p. 15.

46. Laidlaw, Robert H. – A misunderstanding about the year of Laidlaw's birth was corrected in a letter to Mr. Ronald Laidlaw (no relation) dated 9/4/2006 from R.H. Laidlaw's granddaughter, Mrs.Wynn Alexander, and passed to Ian Seeley. She writes – ' ... the sleeve of one of the old vinyl records had my Grandfather's year of birth as 1863, which is incorrect. There was in fact a child born around this time with this name to the same parents, who died in infancy, but my Grandfather was the second child with this name and he was born 24 July 1872 and died 21st January, 1953.' The dates given in the 2001 'The Hawick Songs – A Complete Collection' and its predecessor of 1957 are, in consequence, erroneous and will require alteration in any future edition to 1872-1953.

47. Scottish Student Song Book, The – p. 244 – Bayley & Ferguson, London & Glasgow 1898.

48. Oddy, Zilla – J.E.D. Murray – A Man Of Many Parts – Scottish Borders Council Museum and Gallery Service 1999.

49. Bell, John – Bell was a coachbuilder to trade, born at Ladylaw Place, Hawick on 17th December, 1871. He was a pupil and *protégé* of Walter Fiddes-Wilson (1861-1925), the enterprising organist of St. John's Church, Hawick (1880-91) and afterwards at Wilton. From all accounts, Bell was an outstanding amateur tenor, taking leading solo parts in oratorios, etc. He left Hawick in 1909 to take a post with Scottish Motor Traction (SMT) in Edinburgh and died there in 1941.

50. Stoker, John – in the Monthly Chronicle of Northern Country Lore and Legend, April, 1888 – pp. 170, 171.

51. Hawick Archaeological Society Transactions 1950 – obituary of William Scott Robson.

52. Curwen, John – Curwen (1816-1880) was an English Congregational minister who developed the Tonic-Sol-fa system of reading and sight reading vocal music. By the mid-1860s the widespread acceptance of his system was such that he abandoned the ministry to concentrate on further development – which included the setting up of the Tonic Sol-fa College in London in 1879. The uptake of the 'new notation' (d r m f s etc.) was particularly strong in Hawick with its abundance of churches and very committed choirs. Choral singing was a big thing in Hawick in the Nineteenth Century and William Robson became the town's most ardent Tonic Sol-fa adherent. The Tonic Sol-fa method was prevalent in Hawick until well after the Second World War. Ian Seeley discovered when he arrived in Hawick in 1970 that a number of the members of the very competent choir he inherited at Trinity Church could only read from Sol-fa notation, in the absence of which he was obliged to scribe above staff notation for those who required it.

53. On 26th June, 1918, King George V ordered members of the Royal Family to drop German titles. The Saxe-Coburg dynasty would henceforth become the House of Windsor.

54. The 1861 Census gives a John Rutherford, aged 36, as a journeyman shoemaker. This man is obviously too old to be the song writer and too young to be his father but the similarity of name and occupation is striking and he may well be an uncle.

55. Fiddes-Wilson, Walter (1861-1925) – One of the most enthusiastic, enterprising 'home-grown' Hawick musicians of the Victorian/ Edwardian period. Son of John Fiddes-Wilson, wool merchant, of Leaburn, Hawick, he abandoned the textile trade to study music in Italy. As conductor of Hawick Sacred Harmonic Society, he was courageous in mounting large-scale performances of choral works of the great masters in the Exchange. He started the first amateur operatic organisation in Hawick – Hawick Amateur Opera Company – in 1897. He was organist of St. John's Church, Hawick 1880-1891 and thereafter organist of Wilton Church where his brother-in-law, the Rev. John Rudge Wilson, was minister.

56. Hawick News 29/4/1910 – Report of funeral oration (19/4/1910) for Joshua Taylor by the Rev. John Rudge Wilson.

57. Groome, Francis H. – Note on *Teribus* in The Ballad of Hornshole and the Fight of 1514 – pub. Adam Grant 1914.

58. Ibid.

59. Matthew Robert Smith Craig, MA, LLB (Edin.) – advocate and poet. Born in Hawick 1867. Emigrated to Australia 1899-1905; thereafter lived in south of England and died in Chobham, Surrey 1921. Buried in Wellogate Cemetery, Hawick.

60. Craig, R. S. – In Borderland – Border and Other Verses – pp. 96-99 J. & W. Kennedy, Hawick 1922, first published 1898.

61. Scots Magazine, The – January, 1983, pp. 373-376 – But Who Was James Booth? Article by his daughter, Joyce Booth, explains the Thomson connection and the role of Hawick Exchange. Her father was on tour, as musical director, with Miss. Emma Stanley, a Victorian Joyce Grenfell, who gave a one-woman performance (in which she impersonated 36 different characters) at the Exchange on 10th February, 1873. She surmises that this could be when he first met James Thomson. *The Star of Robert Burns* was first performed in Graham's Hotel, Hawick on 24th January, 1879 at Hawick Burns Club's celebration of the Bard. The Hawick Express 25/1/1879 reports – 'The following song (words printed), composed for the occasion, was well rendered by Mr. Thos. Strathearn.' James Thomson was in the Chair. Booth was a native of Congleton, Cheshire. D. C. Thomson Publications, Dundee 1983.

62. Jessie Easton Murray married George Hall Grant at St. John's Manse, Hawick, 9th October, 1914. She sang at the Colour Bussing of 1919 but, within a year, had joined her husband in Niagara Falls, Canada, where they lived out the remainder of their lives.

63. Hawick Express 31/3/1905 – Report of Callants' Club Dinner, 24/3/1905 in the Tower Hotel, Hawick.